4801428

TOLEDANO

The Franciscan
of Bourges

940·547

Please renew/return this item by the last date shown.

So that your telephone call is charged at local rate,
please call the numbers as set out below:

	From Area codes 01923 or 0208:	From the rest of Herts:
Renewals:	01923 471373	01438 737373
Enquiries:	01923 471333	01438 737333
Minicom:	01923 471599	01438 737599

L32b

− 9 JUL 2003

1 4 MAY 2005

6/12

L 33

D1422670

THE FRANCISCAN OF BOURGES

The Franciscan of Bourges in 1944

Fr.

THE
FRANCISCAN OF BOURGES
by
MARC TOLÉDANO

Translated from the French by
B. B. Rafter and Heather Cremonesi

GEORGE G. HARRAP & CO. LTD
London · Toronto · Wellington · Sydney

First published in Great Britain 1970
by GEORGE G. HARRAP & CO. LTD
182 High Holborn, London, W.C.1

French edition © *Flammarion, Paris* 1967
English translation © *George G. Harrap & Co. Ltd* 1970

SBN 245 59419 1

Composed in Intertype Baskerville type and printed by
Western Printing Services Ltd, Bristol
Made in Great Britain

To the memory of my mother.

To the memory of all the Bordiot prisoners who died for France.

To my friends,
Heinz-Walter Kiepe, who worked with all his heart for Franco-German reconciliation,

Colonel Tommy Macpherson, a Scotsman parachuted to the maquis in the Auvergne, hero of the French Resistance.

The greatest deeds need be but simply told,
Grandiloquence doth mar them.

LA BRUYÈRE
Les Caractères, Chapter V

INTRODUCTION

It may help the reader to understand the full significance of this account if he tries to imagine what it was like to live in France under the German occupying forces from 1940 to 1944, and if he tries to identify himself with those who refused to submit to Hitler's 'new order'.

By the June of 1940 the French were thrown into a state of total confusion. Millions had become refugees. There was a mass exodus from France. The highways seethed with people on the move. They were under constant Stuka fire. They were forever colliding with and extricating themselves from herds of panicking cattle and the transport-columns of a routed army. The country fell apart at the seams. There was no leadership and no government. The Germans swarmed all over the place, instilling terror wherever they went. It was the greatest catastrophe in French history.

The majority of the French army was siphoned off to German prisoner-of-war camps. Most soldiers went before they had as much as fired a single shot at the enemy. Of these 1,850,000 men, some 1,600,000 were sent to Germany in the first three months. They were the mainstay, the defence and strong arm of the nation. They included some 35,000 regular troops and 170 generals. France was drained of her most able, socially competent labour force. Every profession and social level was stunted. Never in the history of mankind had any conquering nation removed and made use of such a vast quantity of highly skilled labour as Nazi Germany did in the summer of 1940.

Vanquished France was sliced into two zones. The Southern Zone was not occupied by German troops and was theoretically a sovereign state governed by Marshal Pétain and Pierre Laval. The Vichy Government was increasingly regulated by German control. Armistice commissions were set up everywhere. People and goods entering or leaving the so-called "Free Zone" came

[7]

under closer and closer German police scrutiny and were eventually subject to German permits. The northern line of the Free Zone was a true frontier with military guards, regular patrols, police dogs, and customs officials.

The Northern Zone was occupied by the German army and administered by it, and a curfew was enforced. This Northern Zone was itself subdivided into two zones. The Forbidden Zone comprised twelve northern and eastern *départements*, the most populous, the richest, and most industrialized areas of the country. Refugees from this zone were not allowed to return home. The Germans gradually colonized the zone by settling their own farmers on the land. This was particularly true of the Ardennes, which became a veritable German agricultural colony. Hitler set up the *Ostland* organization, which saw to the distribution of the arable land that "the French had abandoned and which now should prosper in our capable hands". It seemed from this that Hitler wanted to create a sort of modern Lotharingia, a Flemish state which would include Holland, Belgium, and French Flanders.

Lastly there was Alsace-Lorraine, which was simply annexed to Germany in violation of the armistice terms. The French language was banished along with French books, which were burnt in huge bonfires. German race laws were then applied to the Jews of Alsace-Lorraine. A census was taken and the Jews were made to wear armbands bearing the Star of David, before being deported to the death camps. Alsace-Lorraine's 75,000 soldiers were imprisoned, then freed as German citizens and conscripted into the German army. Thousands of them lost their lives on the Russian Front for a cause they detested. Street names were Germanized, as well as family surnames. Every trace of the region's French past was eradicated.

In 1940 France was occupied and completely overrun by the colossal German army, which requisitioned, looted, and sucked the country dry. France was made to pay huge sums of money by way of war reparation, and French workers were conscripted into German labour camps. Goering appropriated a large quantity of French works of art. Civilian road traffic was banned, families were broken up and scattered, and food was rationed to subsistence level. The flourishing black-market racket was

[8]

allowed, if not officially encouraged, by the occupying forces because it played havoc with the country's economy. The army of
occupation brought an even worse menace in its wake: the
Gestapo. Its members arrived in their hundreds. By the time
they hit France they had had plenty of training and experience
in the Jewish pogroms and Communist purges in Germany and
Poland. These black-uniformed individuals did not cause much
of a stir initially. They went about their work unobtrusively.
They compiled lists of suspects and took note of any "anti-social"
elements such as Jews and Communists. Arrests were made
quietly, at dawn, "with the milk round". The Gestapo used the
critical month of occupation to put out its feelers, to observe,
and set up its organization in large towns.

The French Resistance had not yet been created. The country
was too confused by her defeat to think of resistance. Everyone's
energies were spent on trying to keep body and soul together and
adapt to the new disorders. A very small number of Frenchmen,
which included, however, every single able-bodied man on the
Ile de Sein, answered General de Gaulle's call to join Free
France. Many made it across the Channel to England. The first
intelligence missions were organized in London, and the bare
bones of the future Resistance movement began to rattle into
action as early as July 1940. But they were all isolated efforts,
with no co-ordination. The Resistance had yet to get off the
ground. It took Great Britain's example of "sticking it out"
against Goering's air armadas, and the defeat of the Italian
army in Greece and Africa, and Leclerc's epic battles near Lake
Chad, and General de Gaulle's constant appeals, to make the
French realize that the Germans were not invincible and that
"if France had lost a battle she had not lost the war". At the
end of 1940 there occurred the first anti-German demonstrations.
They were peaceable at first, like the eleventh of November procession to the Arc de Triomphe. These were followed by the first
mass arrests and the first death sentences. Those sinister posters
proclaiming executions and seizure of hostages began to appear on
notice-boards. The first underground networks and movements
were formed. Free French operators penetrated the occupied
territories and sent back radio messages, arms were parachuted
down to Resistance groups, and the first Resistance news-sheets

[9]

began to circulate underground. The Gestapo retaliated with fierce counter-measures. There were mass round-ups, hostages were shot, networks were uncovered and wiped out. Torture was used. The whole country became restive and resolute in their determination to throw off the oppressors, though there were exceptions—the "collaborators" and a few Fascist groups (Darnand, Déat, Luchaire, de Brinon), who bowed to the German jackboot.

When Hitler invaded Russia the French Resistance took courage and the whole underground movement was pulled into shape. Resistance officers in the army set up at the armistice started to store ammunition and arms in the Free Zone. A secret army was also formed. Many still escaped to London and Africa and other countries to rally round de Gaulle. The Gestapo infiltrated Resistance groups with agents, which resulted in more and more networks being smashed. Prisons filled up, millions were deported to death camps, and thousands were executed by firing squads at Mont Valérien, Vincennes, Montluc, Fort Ha, and Bourges. The Gestapo refined and applied torture (bathtub immersions, electrocution, nail ripping, hanging by the feet, and so on) worthy of the Dark Ages.

The Allied landings in North Africa in November 1942 marked the turning-point of the Resistance movement. The Germans retaliated by invading the Free Zone and doing away with the fiction of an independent Vichy regime. The whole of France was thus occupied and subject to Hitler's Third Reich. The Gestapo took over every prison in the land. The youth of France reacted by rushing off to the various battle fronts, to the Tunisian campaigns in North Africa, to Italy, to the liberation of Corsica, to the Provençal landing, to join the Leclerc Division in its stupendous advance from Lake Chad to Berchtesgaden, via England. The Frenchmen who left France to join the army in North Africa faced the hostile Pyrenees, the treachery of men on the frontier who let them through only to trap them, Franco's vile gaols at Miranda, Jacca, Pampeluna, and elsewhere. Many ended up in the hands of the Gestapo, to be sent to Germany never to return. The Nazis also introduced a compulsory labour scheme (the STO), which forced all young Frenchmen to work in Germany, for hands were needed in their munitions factories.

[10]

The first maquis[1] were organized in the Vercors hills, on the Glières plateau, in the Ain, the Jura, and round Limoges and Nevers. The maquis men were heroes. At one time, at Glières, the maquis was surrounded and heavily outnumbered. They fought on until they ran out of ammunition, and only then did they surrender.

The closer the country got to liberation, the harsher became the enemy's counter-measures. After the Normandy landings of June 6th, 1944, the maquis and Resistance multiplied their sallies and attacks on German reinforcements. The SS and the Gestapo retaliated by losing what little control they had; they tore round the countryside setting fire to buildings, hanging people, executing, shooting at random, torturing: witness the incidents at Oradour-sur-Glane, Ascq, Tulle, and Saint-Dié. In that June of 1944 10,000 people were imprisoned, many of whom were deported. Paris Jews were rounded up in a gigantic panic raid and packed off to the Auschwitz ovens.

Liberation dawned over an impoverished nation picked clean of its assets. Scores of towns had been destroyed and damaged in the Franco-German battles or by Allied bombing. The French rose to join in the final war encounters, as members of either the American Forces or the Leclerc Division of the First French Army.

France paid heavily for the War. Tens of thousands of men died in action between 1940 and 1945, and thousands of civilians were killed in air-raids, on firing ranges, and in concentration camps.

This book is dedicated to the prisoners of Bourges detained in the terrible Bordiot Prison, to the men who were helped by Alfred Stanke, the German Franciscan warder, to the men who were deported to Germany and to those who never returned.

Alfred Stanke, the Franciscan of Bourges, was born in Danzig in 1904. He was the sixth child in a family of eleven children, ten of whom were boys. His mother and father were both of Polish origin, like many people on the Baltic coast, which has always been a melting-pot of East and North European nationalities, of Poles, Finns, Swedes, Lithuanians, Varangians, Tartars,

[1] See Translators' Notes, p. 173.

[11]

and Slavs. The family name was Stanicevski. Alfred's father's greatest ambition was to become an engine driver, and he could think of no better profession for his sons. He was prepared to make all manner of sacrifices to achieve this end, which included Germanizing his name to Stanke, because the Prussian Railways Board would not employ men with Polish surnames.

The Stanicevskis were practising Roman Catholics and brought their children up as good Catholics. When Alfred was thirteen he decided he wanted to be a Franciscan, a vocation also chosen by four of his brothers, while his only sister became a Franciscan nun. In 1920, when he was sixteen, Alfred wanted to enter the Breslau seminary, the largest in the area, but his father could not afford to finance his studies. The lad was asked to pay his own way, so Alfred attended a nursing course at Coblenz and at Darmstadt in a hospital run by religious orders. It was at Darmstadt that he became a member of the Third Order of St Francis attached to the Heidelberg Community. When he was twenty he went to Rome as a cook to Pope Pius XI. He learnt some Italian while he was there, and was known as Alfredo. After spending two years at the Vatican he was appointed male nurse to the St Marien Hospital in Cologne, where he remained until the War broke out.

Alfred Stanke had never done any military service. In September 1939 he was sent on a crash course in order to become a medical orderly in the army. In July 1940 he entered occupied France in the service of a German major at the Melun garrison. One day, in September 1940, he happened to meet Brother Franz Stock on a platform of the Gare St Lazare in Paris, the same Franz Stock who was later chaplain at Fresnes Prison and who did so much to comfort and console the hundreds of Resistance men who were shot on the infamous range at Mont Valérien. This chance meeting had a profound effect on Alfred. They had a long talk. Private Stanke, the humble Franciscan orderly from Danzig, was dazzled and awestruck by Franz Stock's impressive personality, by his admiration and knowledge of French culture, by his anti-Nazism, and by his hatred of violence. The two men met frequently over the next few months. Brother Stock told Alfred of his qualms of conscience, of the moral dilemmas which his work, his genuine patriotism, and

[12]

his Christian convictions all provoked. He had a very great influence on Alfred, leading him to a better understanding of France and the French, which helped Alfred to appreciate their needs and problems.

So, when Corporal Stanke was posted to Bourges prison in April 1942 as medical orderly and warder, he thought it quite natural and in order that he should devote himself to his prisoners and become a "secret agent of brotherly love" in the true spirit of St Francis of Assisi.

I was not prompted to write this account of my War-time experiences by any desire to describe the cruelty and barbarity of the Gestapo and their maltreatment and torture of my brother Yves and myself. Many others underwent far greater sufferings, and many had to pay for their patriotic impulses with their lives.

It is a truism that good and evil can and do co-exist, that flowers can and do grow among thistles. It is just as true that the same uniform can clothe a torturer as well as a good man. It has been my intention to demonstrate how a humble German Franciscan monk, Alfred Stanke, could, at the risk of losing his own life, do so much good amid so much evil. He extended his Christian brotherly love to my brother and to me and to hundreds of other French prisoners. He shared with us all his own personal love of humanity. I hope that this account may also help to repay a part of the immense debt of gratitude I owe him.

When the War broke out we were very young and inexperienced. If the first few chapters of the book betray a certain naïve brashness, a lack of responsibility and maturity, it is because I have tried to show how we came to be caught up in the dramatic turn of events while not really understanding their import and gravity. Had my brother and I had any idea of the trials that were in store for us I wonder and even doubt if we should have had the courage to face them. "If my flesh knew now whither my heart would lead it, it would in no time rend itself to shreds," said Gaston de Foix on the eve of the Battle of Ravenna.

Courage is often a synonym for ignorance.

It may well have been our very unconcern and inexperienced

youthfulness which roused Brother Alfred's brotherly love for us. Surrounded as he was by human misery, he was bound instinctively to turn to those who called out for his help. His help gave us the moral assistance we needed to survive the ordeal, and had we not had him we would surely have died. The most important realization that arose from our experiences, more important even than his actual generosity and care for our welfare, was that beneath all the hatred and violence, and within an enemy heart, lay compassion.

It all begin towards the end of the hot summer of 1943 at the spa of Bourbon-l'Archambault. During the Occupation no-one ever went to that peaceful oasis, and not a single German had been seen there since the day France had surrendered. It was a remote outpost of a ravaged country where one could still obtain food without ration cards.

My brother Yves, our cousin Claude Delescure, and I had all decided to take a holiday in a large house in the area which belonged to one of our uncles. We were delighted to be together for the first time since the War broke out. I was two years older than Claude, who was twenty-four, as was Yves. He had been demobilized from the Air Force when the Free Zone disappeared. We all wanted to "do something" which would release us from the inaction that held France in a stranglehold.

The occupation weighed more and more heavily on everyone; the War seemed to be going on for ever. Early-morning arrests and deportations were on the increase. The hopes that had risen out of the events of 1942 and the early part of 1943—the attempted landing at Dieppe, the El Alamein victory, the invasion of North Africa, Stalingrad, the surrender of the Afrika Korps—had all been dashed when the expected liberation did not follow on.

Claude's experience of the War had come to an abrupt end in 1940, and he was raring to get back into active service. The only hope a regular officer had of getting back was to find a way of going to North Africa, but unfortunately we were not in touch with the channels that arranged this sort of enterprise. Then we heard that a friend of ours had been arrested while crossing the Pyrenees, and we became wary. Claude, however, did get his chance. He made contact with an Allied network and threw himself into the business of espionage. He informed the

British Intelligence Service of enemy airfields, and of the number and types of aircraft, anti-aircraft equipment, and defence systems.

Yves had tasted battle in the May of 1940 when he was a corporal in the hussar regiment of General de Gaulle's Armoured Division in the Aisne, near Laon. On May 21st he was riding on the Marle–Guise road in a brand-new motorcycle combination he and his lieutenant had just acquired when the lieutenant shouted at him, "For God's sake sit down, you damn' fool. They'll blast your silly head off!"

My brother continued to stand up in his side-car, partly out of bravado and partly because he did not realize just how dangerous it was. A bullet from a German heavy machine-gun shattered his arm and so interrupted his military career. He retreated from hospital to hospital as the French Army withdrew in full rout, always on the move with all the refugees and always under constant Stuka fire.

Those gruesome days had left Yves with a nagging sense of frustration.

"All I succeeded in doing was to get myself shot up at the age of twenty-one before I had a chance of doing a damned thing," he would say, "and for that they gave me the Croix de Guerre."

My only contact with the War was limited to a brief exposure in May 1940 when I left the Cavalry School at Saumur. I was, however, taken prisoner and put securely behind barbed-wire.

My time in Germany had a profound effect on me. Like most of my generation I was totally unprepared for war, and still less for defeat and captivity. It was nothing like my rather uneventful student life. Nor did those Monday afternoons spent training at the École Militaire Supérieure prepare any of us for modern warfare. They were a good excuse for meeting our friends from the Faculties of Law and of Political Science. We would all make an evening of it after doing a bit of work-out in the courtyard of the École Militaire, or an arms drill with hilariously anachronistic weapons like the sabre, the carbine, or the Lebel rifle. Nor had my crash course at Saumur made me any the readier.

The spirit of Munich had hoodwinked many of us. I did not

think there would be a war, and the awakening was thus the ruder.

I was the youngest in the Oflag at Nuremberg and had the most junior rank, that of cadet officer. The captive officers rather looked down their noses at aspiring cadets. We were the dregs, their poor cousins—not quite officers and yet not NCOs, and in either case not fitting company. I fumed at the futility of this captivity and spent my time there in a state of frustrated revolt. The only thing I thought of was escaping and returning to fight in France. I wanted to be part of the preparations then afoot for the liberation, to be on the crest of the wave and not in the trough I was then in. I longed to be in on the making of history. Every twenty-three-year-old man would resent the way these officers settled down to a middle-class existence in their prison environment, resigning themselves to making the best of their lot. While the war was waging in Eritrea, Libya, Greece, over London, our senior officers seemed to have nothing better to do than wrangle in the Oflag over an extra ladleful of soup, over precedence and seniority at the theatre and in Sanskrit classes. Others were sticklers for kit inspections in the hut, for hospital-corners on beds. German propaganda did not help; we were bombarded with emasculating slogans like "We are here to expiate the mistakes of the Third Republic", "It was our side which declared war", "The Führer offered us friendship", or "A prison camp is a school for the soul."

Barbed wire has never redeemed anyone. A prisoner-of-war camp like the one at Nuremberg is but a replica of a village with ten thousand inhabitants, all male, mirroring the same old virtues, vices, and problems shared by free men, only exacerbated by promiscuity. The good remained good and the bad remained bad. Some became mystics; homosexuals indulged themselves; armchair strategists conceived of campaigns, and so on. It was not necessarily the law of the jungle that predominated, but rather a dictatorship of petty nastiness.

Whenever I broached the subject of escape there was some fossilized officer, the kind who wins wars from behind a desk, to come wagging a finger at me, saying, "Escape my foot. All you want to do is run back to your slippers."

Who ever thought of slippers at the age of twenty-three!

[17]

I did try it in 1941. I trudged some two hundred miles through the forests and fields and country lanes of the Third Reich, until I was caught by police dogs at the Swiss border.

Then, in June 1943, I got out in a curious way. I was swapped by a shifty German doctor for a large quantity of sausage and other such delicacies. I was then working as an interpreter in the Hammelburg Stalag kitchens in Franconia after doing a stint in the disciplinary companies, in the labour camps, and on the work farms in Württemberg. The fellow in charge of the kitchens was an old anti-Nazi, pro-French officer who took a liking to me. This colourful old gentleman was called Horeyzeck and he and the shady doctor were thick as thieves. They had worked out a system for putting kitchen staff on the sick list. Their treatment benefited them both and went like this: "I'll give you some sausage and bacon if you'll get a cook invalided out."

The simple swap was made complicated in my case because I looked so healthy. I had been among the pots and pans for ten months when Horeyzeck put me up for barter. The doctor was not interested. My chief doubled the amount of sausage, and threw in a ham and a bacon joint, but both to no avail. The major could not be persuaded. This initiated a series of involved negotiations conducted in great secrecy behind closed doors, which went on for a good fortnight. Helmut Schoeller, an NCO who was in on the whole thing, told me quite a lot of what went on. "The whole thing is hilarious. The major wants more and more every day. He pushes up his pound of flesh and eggs the poor old man on and on. He'll soon have your entire weight in blood sausage, bacon, and hams."

In fact, this did not strike me as being such a bad idea. Everyone would probably be delighted if the Germans swapped their million and a half French prisoners for an equivalent weight of pig-meat.

Every morning and every evening we would see the major slinking out of the office with a parcel of savoury sausage tucked under his arm. He would creep off, slinking along the walls like some guilty ghost, all of which was wasted effort as he fooled no-one. He was always in a state of intense excitement; actually, I think he was probably slightly mad. He had been a psychiatrist

[18]

in civilian life, and some of his patients' eccentricities must have rubbed off on to him, which would explain his odd behaviour.

A carton of Red Cross chocolate finally broke down his resistance. Then there was the last hitch: we had to find some near-valid medical reason for my release. An old wound in my foot seemed to fit the bill until the medical officer decided the scar was too good. I would have to make it fester a bit before I went before the Medical Discharge Board. I agreed reluctantly to jab at the scar with a pronged kitchen fork. After three rounds of foot-pronging I decided I'd had enough. A whole ham and two dozen eggs put an end to the farce, and I soon found myself among a train-load of homeward-bound invalids. I kept up a good limp for the sake of appearances, only to notice that three-quarters of those on board were about as sick as my foot.

When the train finally pulled out I thought I was on my way home. But General Giraud chose to escape from his fortress the very day we left Hammelburg, and so everything went wrong. When we got to the French border everything seemed to be going smoothly, and our various afflictions miraculously began to disappear. Then our carriages were uncoupled and we returned from whence we came. The German guards did not explain our mystery train tour, and so we jogged along in blissful ignorance. We woke up behind barbed wire in the Petrisberg camp at Trier. Hitler had decided to dump us there as a reprisal for Giraud's escape. We feigned sick were in trouble for we would now have to reappear before the Discharge Board, which would inevitably send us back to hard-labour camps. I was very lucky. The camp commandant mistook the cavalry badge on my greatcoat collar for that of the medical corps and so took me for a doctor. I did my daily rounds in this guise, struggling to keep a straight face, applying my stethoscope, looking professionally grave as I administered doses of aspirin. It was the only medicine I had, and even if my patients did not make remarkable recoveries, at least my cures could do them no harm. I had to keep this up for seven months. My patients gradually disappeared to the various Kommandos. My medical duties protected me against any unpleasant surprises. At the end of June 1943 the remnants of the Hammelburg contingent were at last returned to France.

I was demobilized and tried to settle down to civilian life in a country which had changed beyond recognition: occupied, hungry, looted, drained by the enemy. My life in the Northern Zone seemed so dreary and pointless that I decided to go to the so-called Free Zone, where one of my uncles lived, to see whether things were any better there. It was a revelation. I met a former fellow-student from the School of Political Sciences who was chief assistant to a minister. He took me to Vichy, where he introduced me to various senior officials attached to ministries, or organizing committees as they were known. The kind of organizing these young men excelled at was seeing to it that they had plenty of food for themselves from the farms in the Allier. This whole busy group of men took themselves deadly seriously, strutting self-importantly through a fictitious existence in the sham capital of a so-called sovereign state. They spent their days framing orders and laws in the bathrooms-cum-offices of their requisitioned hotels, between the bidet and the wash-basin. The whole set-up made me sick—the mystique of the Marshal and the National Revolution, the swarms of uniforms (when perhaps it would have been more fitting to be discreet about such things), and the blatant proliferation of posters and slogans inspired by Nazi propaganda. They all seemed to have lost sight of the vital issues: the country was under the jackboot; there was still a war on; and there was such a thing as Free France.

This experience redoubled my resolve to take an active part in shaping coming events. I was soon to find myself involved . . . though not, unfortunately, in the way I had hoped.

My cousin Claude entrusted his first mission to Yves on September 1st, 1943. It seemed quite straightforward—to find out what defences there were at the Châteauroux and Avord aerodromes, near Bourges, and how many planes they had on the ground. Claude had impressed upon Yves the necessity of memorizing all the information and never writing anything down. I do not know why, but Avord aerodrome frightened me. It may have been because the base was an important one for Germany and thus extremely well guarded. Yves's incredible temerity and his light-hearted disregard for danger also terrified me, and made me wish I was going in his stead.

[20]

When Yves left on September 1st, his ears buzzing with sound advice, I suddenly felt that something awful was going to happen. He stayed at the Hôtel du Cygne at Châteauroux and by the following morning he was in a position to do his work. He was right on the edge of the base at La Martinerie, three miles from the town. He strolled casually about among the gorse, counting the Messerschmitts as they landed, and noted a dozen anti-aircraft guns. After he had been wandering around like a leisurely tourist for a couple of hours, and having encountered no-one, he decided to go on to Avord. Châteauroux had been child's-play. There was obviously no need to be cautious and wary. He sat down under a hedge and ate a sandwich, then, realizing there was nothing and no-one to stop him, he went onto the airfield. He wandered along a disused runway, came upon the empty hangars, and began to count the marker beacons, and the Heinkel 111s as they screamed off the tarmac. He tried to estimate the acreage of the aerodrome—which no-one had asked him to do—but finding it beyond him, he made a rough sketch of the base in his notebook. Then everything started happening at once. Rounding a bend bordered by hedges, he bumped into a soldier in battledress holding his rifle in his left hand, his right buttoning up his trousers. The man seemed somewhat embarrassed by the encounter, as if he had been caught doing something he shouldn't. My brother pretended he had lost his way after answering a similar call of nature.

"You can explain that at the guardroom," the soldier replied. "I'm only obeying orders."

The German made Yves climb up into a lorry full of soldiers in transit to the other end of the field. The men took him for a French worker at the camp and paid not the slightest attention to him. Yves desperately tried to think of ways of ridding himself of the fatal notebook, or of tearing out the incriminating page and swallowing it, but he could do nothing under the vigilant eye of the NCO.

When he got to the guardroom he was not investigated very thoroughly. He was searched, of course, and his notebook was taken away along with his other things, and he was then put into an army cell. He was in the charge of a decent, chatty old territorial who looked harmless. He spent the day in the company of the bewhiskered *Feldgrau*, playing cards, sharing his meal, and talking about Germany. Yves cheated wildly as they played, but his gaoler was so nice to him that it became embarrassing. My brother wanted to overpower the fellow, put on his uniform, and make a quick getaway, but he had no way of doing this.

"There's no point, really," he thought. "I'll be out in twenty-four hours."

When his door was unlocked next morning he was convinced they had come to release him. But behind his gaoler was a civilian dressed in green, his face hidden by a green hat pulled down low on his head. Then handcuffs snapped shut round Yves's wrists.

He was bundled into one of those front-wheel-drive Citroëns the Gestapo always used. A police dog sat next to the driver and a tall, thin SS man with a face like a skunk kept a sharp eye on Yves. My brother tried to talk to the man, only to have a peremptory "Shut up!" spat at him. This did not augur well. Things looked as though they were taking an even worse turn when the car stopped in a side-street in Bourges, and Yves was pushed into the Gestapo headquarters.

The investigation got under way immediately with a few opening kicks in the shins and clouts across the face. The tall, thin man in spectacles had Yves's notebook in his hands and knew what he was after. My brother made up a complicated story with explanations which soon contradicted themselves. The Gestapo man was not to be fooled. He sent for two colleagues who, when they arrived, looked like a couple of real thugs. The interrogation then began in earnest. Yves thrashed about in self-defence, trying to protect his head. He even managed to take a good bite out of a hairy fist that came within range. They really set about him properly then. He was bound hand and foot, hurled onto the floor, booted, stamped on, beaten up. He confessed—not the truth, of course, but a story that might hold water, involving parachute drops, the maquis in the Berry, gun-running, and sabotage.

His tormentors were not very sharp and they seemed pleased with this version. Yves's confession was serious enough to warrant the gallows but he had betrayed nothing and no-one, and that was the main thing. He was given a bowl of soup and a cigarette, and a lecture which somehow linked Hitler, Joseph Darnand, the New Order, and, of all people, Joan of Arc. Yves was too punch-drunk to make any sense of it all.

It was late at night when he was carted off to the Bordiot, where he had to go through endless committal procedures.

The following morning two henchmen of Fritz Schultz, the Gestapo man who had directed his interrogation, took my brother from his cell. One of them, Ernst Basedow, who had a pair of steely eyes set in a large, red face, was beside himself with anger. Brandishing a bunch of keys, he blared out, "You've lied to us, you bloody pig. You'll pay for that, you will. If we don't get the truth this time, we'll rip your bleeding guts out."

Yves was shoved into the black Citroën, was taken away, and was eventually put into a small dungeon barely large enough for an undersized midget. He stewed away there for a good hour, and then he was brought before the chief, who hissed at him in German, "Your story doesn't add up. We're not fools, you know."

This session started with a series of wallops administered with a lead-filled hose-pipe. There were variations: there were blows from a steel ruler, riding-crop beatings, various kicks and punches. Yves made up another even less likely story laced with all sorts of incredible detail. He signed his second confession and was taken back to his cell.

On the third day an even more foul-tempered Basedow collected Yves as he tumbled out of his bunk. He could hardly stand now. He was physically quite broken and his brain felt soggy. He could no longer understand the questions posed by the three Gestapo men. The one thing he managed to realize was that he had to try to keep talking, to say anything that came into his head in an effort to ward off the blows. He got himself hopelessly lost in a maze of new detail, and kept contradicting a wildly improbable story peopled by all sorts of invented characters. He was caught out by the very efforts he made to allay detection: they understood he was leading them by the nose. Their grip never relaxed for a second; the rain of blows increased, and they took it in turns to beat him up.

Suddenly, Yves felt everything inside him let go and give. Self-preservation took over and he confessed the truth. While he was speaking he was aware of a total split within his person. His body was forcing his tongue to speak, while another part of his consciousness was passing judgment on his betrayal of Claude. This happened when Schultz and his men strung him up from one of the beams in the cellar. The lynching was done with macabre ritual—they threw up a new hemp rope, made a show of testing it for strength, and pulled aggrieved faces while Schultz started intoning mock prayers and Basedow and another SS man crossed themselves grotesquely.

Yves was convulsing. He was swallowing his swollen tongue: he was being strangled. Sweat started streaming down his chest and a deathly noise almost shattered his ear-drums as his arteries pounded at a pulse-rate of at least a hundred and forty. As he hung there Ernst and Schultz and another man were battering him to death. Even the head of the Gestapo joined in with a metal crop.

On the brink of death, Yves confessed.

They threw him back into the undersized dungeon. As he fell, he hit his head against the rough concrete of the back wall and his eyebrow burst open. The blood trickled down over his eyelids and he collapsed on to a heap of logs. One wonders what they were doing there. He sank into a near coma. After a short while he was kicked into consciousness and dragged to another cellar where some special court had convened. Schultz, pale and hunched, presided behind a table, horsewhip in hand, a self-appointed judge. His assistants sat about him in a semi-circle. Yves lay completely trussed up on the courtroom floor.

"Who is the head of the Resistance in the Cher?" Schultz began with feigned innocence.

"I don't know."

Another round of blows rained down on him. He started to make up another story in an effort to put a stop to the beating. "Jean Doyen," he gasped, choosing a name at random.

"Never heard of him. You're lying. All right, let him have it."

A third man and then a fourth appeared before Yves and began to move around him in a sort of tribal scalping dance. They were so close to their victim that they nearly hit each other.

[24]

Yves finally mumbled, "The prefect."

This did not, however, earn him a respite. "Bloody fool," Schultz exploded, and the beating continued.

Then Yves started to go quite mad. He thought he was a spinning top whirling amid the flames of hell, tossed about by the Devil's henchmen who clubbed at his head with their axes. There were a hundred, then a thousand, then ten thousand, all yapping like jackals. Their Alsatian friend, the Cerberus that guarded the door, became a many-headed beast barking encouragement in relays through each set of ghastly jaws. Sparks seemed to fly off the whiplashes amid the floating tufts of flannel and pieces of wool that had been ripped from Yves's clothing.

He came to from his nightmare in the rat-hole, lying against the wall. The key turned again in the lock, the jackboots rang on the cellar stairs, and he was pushed into Schultz's office, ablaze with uniforms and reeking of warm beer and cigar smoke.

The great thug who had given Yves such a pounding stood in the middle of the room with a machine-gun in his hand. Schultz ordered them to shove my brother's back against the wall and tie his hands behind his neck.

"Well, where shall we start, then," roared Ernst, "balls or head?"

"Go for the heart. It'll be quicker."

"Not likely, you bloody fool, we've not finished with you yet. You haven't spilt the beans yet, have you? This is just a foretaste of what you'll get."

The whole room shook with the great burst of laughter that accompanied this, and Yves was taken back to the Bordiot.

Yves was only supposed to have been away for forty-eight hours. By the fifth day we were all very alarmed at Bourbon-l'Archambault. My aunt Andrée could not hide her anxiety, and wished the devil would take these nephews she loved and spoilt and who would be the death of her yet. She wanted to phone anyone in the whole world who could help her to trace Yves's whereabouts. Claude and I were not as pessimistic as she was, but we were still worried. Only Uncle Frédéric kept calm.

On the ninth day we panicked. I phoned every hotel in Châteauroux—not that there were that many. I found out where

[25]

Yves had spent the night of September 1st, a cheap little place. I did not meet with the same luck at Bourges. He had not booked in anywhere.

Claude and I decided we had to go to Bourges, find him, and move heaven and earth to bring him home dead or alive. We were armed only with youthful ingenuousness and a whole lot of illusions. We arrived in Bourges on September 10th, quite late in the evening.

We just managed to find a hotel before the curfew. The town bristled with German troops, mostly airmen from the surrounding bases. We spent the night concocting wild schemes. We came to no real conclusion, but one thing we did realize was that if Yves were in the hands of the Germans there was precious little we could do to rescue him. We finally agreed on the first move: we would see the French police who would tell us where he was. There was a slim chance that he might have been arrested by them. In any case the French police would surely have a list of Frenchmen held by the Germans. We also tried kidding ourselves that my brother had been picked up by the Germans for something like breaking the curfew.

The following morning we went to the barber's to make ourselves look respectable before going to the police. The consequences of this innocent decision were to prove extremely dangerous.

There was only one client in the shop, a German. All we saw of the man beyond the barber's full wrap were a pair of jackboots, a low-browed, square head, and a large area of shaven nape above a horribly lined and folded neck like that of a slaughtered pig on a butcher's slab.

As he sat waiting for his turn, Claude could not help remarking, quite audibly, "God, just look at that revolting stuffed pig. They'd know what to do with him at the Olida ham factory."

I thought him a bit rash, but I wasn't going to be outdone. "You're right. He really takes the cake. He's a perfect Dubout caricature. All that fat neck needs is a piece of adhesive tape."

The German did not move a muscle beneath his lather, but the barber darted us a sideways look full of reproof and anxiety.

When the soldier got up our hearts skipped a beat at the sight

[26]

of his brown uniform, the ominous silver skull on the black background of one of his tunic collars and on the other side the two lozenges that denoted the Security Service. The epaulettes were decorated with the twisted braid worn by officers in the Reich Security Police—in other words, he was a Gestapo big-wig.

"How much do I owe you?" he asked the barber in impeccable French. "Does that include service?"

Before he left the shop he turned his cold, staring eyes on us and, adjusting his cap, said slowly and ominously, "A very good morning to you, gentlemen. I hope I shall have the pleasure of meeting you again soon."

The threatening message was clear. I felt a cold shiver run down my spine and Claude went white.

"You fellows must be crazy," burst out the barber. "He's only one of the heads of the local Gestapo, you know. He got every word you said, and I did too. If you know what's good for you you'll make yourselves scarce. I'll bet you anything you like he'll be round here in five minutes with one of his thugs. If he ever catches sight of you again you'll have had it."

We did not need to be told twice and disappeared immediately, without our haircuts.

The French police kept us waiting an age. They had no information, they were overworked, Yves was not on their list, and they kept telling us to return the following day. We finally slipped a sergeant a five-franc piece and he found out that Yves was in prison at the Bordiot and that he had been arrested on September 3rd.

"If you want any more details you had better apply to the German military tribunal at the Law Courts, opposite the Jacques Coeur Palace."

Now we knew.

I went along to the tribunal by myself—we took the precaution of leaving Claude to wait for me in a café. I was shown before a judge, a Captain Steinmann, whose office was a magnificent medieval room with tapestries and wood-carvings. It really made my blood boil to see this green-uniformed soldier preening himself amid the splendours of the fifteenth-century palace. I thought it best to speak French. The clerk interpreted.

"No, sir," was the answer, "your brother does not appear to

[27]

be down on our prison register. Could you tell me what business he had in Bourges? Can you imagine why he might have been arrested?"

I launched into a cock-eyed explanation, alleging that Yves had gone to visit a construction site near Avord, suggesting he may have forgotten about the curfew, that he may have taken a wrong turning and got lost, that he may have had a row with some German soldiers who had had one too many . . .

"German soldiers don't drink," snapped the judge. "If you wait a moment I'll check and see if your brother is with the Security Service. He may have been arrested by them."

I could not hear what the Gestapo answered on the other end of the line, but when the captain hung up he gave me an odd look.

"As I suspected, your brother was arrested by the Security Police. They would like you to go round to their headquarters on the rue Michel-de-Bourges where they will tell you all you want to know. I'd go round immediately if I were you."

This was the trap and I walked straight into it.

"Surely you're not going to listen to him," Claude said when I joined him at the café. "They'll never let you go and then you'll both be in the soup. It won't do anyone any good. We must all go underground. They'll be after the whole family now."

"No. I've made up my mind. I'm going to get Yves out of there."

"Good Lord, you must still believe in fairies. You can't possibly get him out."

"I know the Germans. I've lived among them long enough to know how to talk them round."

"The ones you knew weren't in the Gestapo. They were like lambs by comparison. These are the genuine article. You can't argue with the Gestapo, they argue with truncheons. Come on, Marc, forget it."

Like most mild people, I can be very stubborn. I had got it into my head that I was going to get Yves out, and nothing could change my mind. The gesture was chivalrous, idealistic, ingenuous, immature, and horribly rash.

"I've made up my mind, Claude. I'm going to the Gestapo."

I must have been a complete jumble of emotions at that time.

[28]

The decision was made out of a desire to indulge in extravagant gestures, to court real dangers and expose myself to new and terrible experiences. Anyway, I vastly overestimated my powers.

"Have it your way then," said Claude, "but I think you're out of your mind—you're actually choosing to walk into the lion's den. Well, if that's want you want to do, let's at least have a brandy together. It'll cheer us up a bit. It's three o'clock now. If you're not back by five this evening, I shall be off. Things will be getting too hot for me around here. Cheers, then, and bloody good luck."

"I'm not going to say goodbye, Claude, but see you later."

We shook hands warmly and I left.

The rue Michel-de-Bourges is near the great mass of St Stephen's Cathedral. It is a short, narrow little street. I had no difficulty finding the Gestapo HQ. A stony-faced SS sentry, tommy-gun in hand, stood by the door. The forbidding aspect of the place, with its barred windows and the barbed-wire barricade at each end of the street, advertised the presence of the Gestapo. I am sure that few Frenchmen ever went of their own free will to knock at that heavy, cast-iron door.

The closer I drew to the entrance, the more scared I became and the more convinced I was that I was mad to take this risk. No-one in his right mind seeks out the Gestapo, but rather avoids it like the plague. I paused before that SS-black door and my courage deserted me. I must have lifted my arm to ring the bell ten times. The eleventh time I made it. The door swung back silently on its hinges. It was too late now. There was no turning back. I took a couple of hesitant steps forward in the entrance and an automatic spring slammed the door shut behind me. I was in the lion's den.

[II]

In the entrance porch were two huge black mastiffs on guard, chained to their kennels. They growled and woke an Alsatian dozing in a Citroën parked in the courtyard. The dog began to bark.

A bald civilian appeared. "What can I do for you?"

"I am Yves Tolédano's brother. You have arrested him by mistake. I want to speak to your chief."

"Please come through here and wait." He showed me into a room which looked like a doctor's waiting-room. There were magazines on a table and I sat down and flicked through a German illustrated weekly. My fear had disappeared. I felt totally at ease and I was glad to have come.

A few minutes later a jackbooted, brown-uniformed, fair Gestapo giant with steel-blue eyes came in. He stood before me and asked in poor French, "Are you the brother of a man called Yves Tolédano?"

"Yes, I am, I—"

I had no time to continue. He let fly with a straight left which caught me on the chin. Then came a right to my nose, an upper-cut to my temple, and a right hook to the solar plexus. I hurtled back a few yards towards the wall where I was grabbed in an arm-lock, while three beefy men materialized out of thin air and bound my ankles and manacled my wrists behind my back. It was a superbly organized and timed assault.

"Ach," said the giant to his henchmen with a twisted smile of satisfaction, "now we've rounded up *die ganze Saubande* [literally, "the whole gang of sows"]. Search him thoroughly, he may be armed."

Well, they were experts at this: pockets were torn out, shoes and socks shaken, trousers and jacket-lining ripped, seams, lapels, padding slashed, all in a twinkling. My belt, tie, wallet,

address book, packet of cigarettes were all confiscated. While
this was going on the leader pounded away at my face. He must
have been wearing a signet-ring or some sort of knuckle-duster,
because my gums soon burst, my lips split open, and my mouth
was full of blood which started to trickle down my shirt. A swing
to my left eye closed it completely. I crumpled groggily to the
floor. The four of them whisked me on to my feet again and held
me up by the armpits. The reception committee was well drilled.

The punches came faster when they found a cigarette holder
with an ejection spring and a nicotine filter in one of my pockets.
The numbskulls became all excited thinking it was a midget
grenade thrower, or a poison pen, or a cyanide syringe.

"Watch it," said one of them, "it's dangerous. It's that new
English weapon."

I couldn't help mumbling at them through my swollen lips,
"It's for putting cigarettes in, you damn' fools!"

That really annoyed them and earned me another pounding
from the flaxen battering-ram.

He soon seemed to tire, or he may perhaps have stopped because he had to go and practise his expertise elsewhere. He lifted
a trap-door in the floor and dropped me down the hole. I slid
down a chute feet first into the basement, and collided violently
with the wall of some special cell. It was pitch dark and there
was no room to stand, sit, or lie, only to crouch, which was
awkward with one's hands bound behind one's back and one's
feet hobbled. I was left to stew in the cramped, dark, damp hole.

My head started to clear. "Where the hell am I? Oh, yes, I
know, I'm in a Gestapo cell. Four lousy swine have just beaten
hell out of me—but I'm still going to walk out of here!"

My body, bruised and battered from the hiding and from the
chute descent, was beginning to hurt considerably. My knees
were very painful and my swollen mouth felt as though I had
been to the dentist. I managed to turn on to my side, and started
to inch about the floor with my head and elbows. One hand
found a container that felt like a flowerpot. My fingers explored
it, but soon withdrew. The pot was full of excrement.

Then I began the tiring job of getting one leg after another
through the chains in order to bring my arms in front of me
again. First I had to get rid of the rope that bound my feet, but

[31]

fortunately it was fairly slack. I would just have to use the filthy chamber-pot. I grabbed it and banged it down. Of course, the slops spilt over me and the stench made me retch. The pot resisted. I banged it down again violently on the stone floor. It yielded and cracked. I felt for a sharp bit and tried to cut the rope. My calves got cramp, as I was bent double against the wall with my legs tucked under me. I gave up dozens of times, only to start again. Salty sweat mingled with the blood and saliva in my mouth. The handcuffs were tearing my wrists. Then I thought I heard something, but it was only my pulse thumping in my head. Breathing was difficult, and I thought my nose must be broken. I kept repeating, "Ernst, you filthy pig, I'll make you pay for this," to keep my spirits up.

Little did I know then that if anyone was going to pay for anything it was going to be me, and a hundredfold.

The rope finally gave to the sound of an ear-piercing, soulless shriek coming from above. It was a woman's cry, the interminable, ghastly death-scream of a slaughtered animal, slowly diminishing, dying away into the silence it had broken. It sounded especially eerie ringing round my hell-hole. I felt terror grip my stomach, and my teeth clattered like so many castanets. Where did that desperate yell come from? What on earth were they doing to that woman? Perhaps they were cutting off her breasts, or she was being impaled. It was a long time before I calmed down, and even then my ears kept ringing with that dreadful, suffering death-cry.

It was comparatively easy to get my arms out in front again, by just slipping the handcuffs under my feet. The next step was harder, but fortunately my small bone-structure made the task easier. The left handcuff was looser than the right, and by dint of stretching my finger joints, contracting my palm, and simultaneously pulling on the handcuff, I forced it along my wrist and hand, ripping off all the hairs as it came. I had one wrist free. I almost yelled for joy. The door was the next obstacle. The wood had small cracks in it, and holes probably made by nails. I looked through one of these holes and realized my hole was a coal-cellar lit by a grill that gave on to the street. A great heap of coal went up almost as far as the grill. I could just distinguish the shadow of the sentry's legs pacing up and down outside. I knew what I had to do. Anything was better than rotting in this airless coal-bunker. I would break down the door, scramble up the coal-heap, and heave myself through the vent. I would deal with the SS man when I got to him.

I began to batter the door, but the confined space and the awkward posture it imposed reduced the possibility of getting any impetus behind my ramming. All I could do was cram my feet into the far corner of the cell and fall sideways on to the door with my shoulder. I felt the wood begin to give a little, and the crack gave me strength. Five more minutes and I am sure the door would have collapsed. But fate had other plans for me. Footsteps sounded on the stairs and a light was switched on. I quickly slipped my left handcuff back on, but I did not have time to get my hands behind my back. The key turned in the lock.

"Get out. Interrogation."

The great chunk of an SS man noticed nothing: neither the damaged door, nor the severed rope, nor the broken chamber-pot. Nor did he react to my hands being in front, though he probably did not know they had originally been behind my back. He pushed me up the stairs before him. As I passed by a window I caught sight of my reflection. I was horrified at the clots of blood round my mouth, at the sight of my bloody, swollen nose and my black eye. It was dark, I noticed. It must have been about eight in the evening. I had arrived about three, which meant I had spent four whole hours in that hole without realizing it.

The SS man sat me down in an office and locked one of my handcuffs to the chair-leg. The head of the Gestapo came in. He was elegantly dressed in a brown suit, and at first sight did not look unpleasant. He was about forty, on the small side, and rather stout, a Mediterranean type. He came from Potsdam and was called Erich Hasse. He studied me in silence. Then a young girl with chestnut-brown hair, hazel eyes, and a slim, graceful figure joined Hasse and sat down at a typewriter.

"Annie, my dear," said her boss, "you can speak French, so ask this louse here what he was up to in Bourges. Don't let him pull the wool over your eyes with his sentimental hogwash. He'll probably tell you how he came to rescue his brother and all that

[33]

sort of shit. He's the same sort of turd as the other one, though he looks even more dangerous to me. I'll leave him to you."

To show me he was a real man and that the girl was his plaything, he kissed her noisily on the mouth, squeezed her breasts a bit, and left.

Marie Fuhrmann, known as Annie,[1] was born at Bitche and was therefore French. She had been a junior typist at the Longwy mines and was now lording it as the all-powerful mistress of Erich Hasse. She stared at me and said nothing while she polished her painted fingernails.

Since providence had given me this lovely-looking inquisitor, I decided to make the best of my good fortune. I would be as charming as I could. I cursed my swollen mouth, bashed-up face, black eye, and ragged clothing. I wasn't exactly looking at my best. But I still had one good eye, and it would just have to do the work of two.

I felt at a disadvantage for two reasons, however: firstly, because I was sitting in a very awkward and humiliating posture, attached to the chair-leg; and secondly, because I did not know how or why Yves had been arrested and—if he had confessed—how much he had said about the Avord mission and Claude's part in it all. I decided to be very careful and keep to generalities.

I decided to make the first move. She was, after all, but a secretary, and I could surely get the better of her. As smoothly as my battered lips permitted, I started.

"Why is it that a pretty young woman like you, with such beautiful eyes, is not busy being a film-star rather than wasting her time as an interpreter in a one-horse town like Bourges?"

"You are here to tell me about your business and not to mind mine," she snapped.

I suppose I had asked for it. I had tried to score too soon and had probably ruined my chances. The girl did, however, blush and lower her eyes. Perhaps she did react to compliments, after all.

"We have good reason to believe that you are the head of the Cher Resistance. So start by telling me what you were up to in Bourges."

[1] Annie Fuhrmann was tried at Dijon in June 1948, and sentenced to four years' imprisonment.

"I know nothing about the Cher Resistance nor about the Resistance anywhere else. I came here to find out why my brother was arrested."

"How did you know he was here?"

"The French police told me."

"That's a lie. We never give them the names of people we arrest."

There was something unpleasant about the way she stressed that "we". I had to make an effort to remember that this young woman was a Gestapo agent. She must have given them proof of her capabilities to have got where she was. The only kind of female I could imagine being part of a torture outfit like this was some coarse brazen tart who swore and behaved like a trooper.

Yet there she was before me, quietly tapping out my replies on her typewriter. She never raised her voice. She spoke excellent French in a perfectly normal tone. I might have been sitting before a typist at my local town hall answering inquiries about my property for a survey map.

"But why on earth should I lie to you in the situation I'm in?"

"You are lying. You were sent here by the Berry terrorists to organize a plot. If you know what's good for you you'll make a clean breast of it all because we have other means of making you talk."

"I give you my word of honour that I know nothing of this terrorist business. I will admit to hoping that Germany will be defeated, but there's nothing odd about that when some forty million Frenchmen hope the same, with the exception of a few traitors."

I did not know then that she was French or I would have said, "with the exception of a few traitors like you."

"You may have to pay dearly for this kind of talk. You strike me as being very cocky and self-assured. As for your word of honour, you can keep it: it's useless."

"You ask me for the truth and when I give it to you, you're not satisfied!"

For over an hour I argued while the lovely Annie played cat and mouse with me. She kept off the subject of Yves and concentrated exclusively on me and my work as leader of a gang of terrorists. She clung tenaciously to this idea of my activities. I fought back gallantly, making veiled passes and getting in a few teasing barbs.

The interview gradually lost its bitterness and one-sidedness, and began to acquire the qualities of a conversation. Only my chained wrist reminded me of my situation. She asked me about my studies and about Paris, and stopped typing out my answers. She casually smoked a cigarette and crossed her legs high up to reveal a good deal of real silk stocking.

I began to think I had won through when her boss returned, and I heard her whisper to him, "I think he's telling the truth and that he isn't involved in this business. If he's lying, which I think is unlikely, he's being incredibly clever."

All my efforts to persuade and flatter her had not been in vain. I had scored a victory—or so I thought—and I returned to my cell feeling quite bucked. I was put into another cell and my arms were secured behind my back. It was slightly larger than the last and I could just stand up, but it was just as narrow and dark. The door was very solid, and I could make no impression on it with my shoulder. I stayed there for a good hour, feeling very thirsty. I kept licking the blood that still oozed from my lips, and my legs began to wobble.

I tried to sort out the avalanche of events that had overtaken me during the last few hours, but my mind was not functioning properly. I was probably too tired. The beatings, which were nothing compared with what awaited me, and then Annie Fuhrmann's interrogation, had taken their toll. My nervous system was functioning in reverse. I was losing my grip. My reasoning powers had slowed down. It was not innocence now but crass ignorance which kept my illusions alive. What a fool I was. It had still not dawned upon me that the Gestapo never recognized the existence of suspects but only of guilty parties. The Gestapo was a hawk holding a twitching field-mouse tenaciously between its talons: it never let go . . .

The SS guard shoved me out of my cell with a rough "Raus . . . Get out!" and made me run up the cellar stairs on the double, the muzzle of his pistol in my ribs. I realized a new chapter was starting in the rue Michel-de-Bourges.

[36]

⌈III⌋

"Where were you on the first of September?"

The question whistled out drily from "Scharführer" Schultz's lips, thin as a sabre's edge.

This Gestapo NCO was really ugly. He looked like a grey sewer-rat. Everything about him was grey, his uniform, his hair, his skin, as if he had spent all his life underground. He had a bony face with cunning, colourless, dead-fish eyes, almost hidden behind the inordinately thick lenses of his spectacles. The Gestapo had outdone itself in finding a specimen like this as an executioner.

Next to him sat big Ernst, straddling a chair. After a few greeting punches, he had settled down to picking his teeth with his penknife. He stared at me like a tiger watching an antelope.

"I don't know," I replied, "I can't remember." Which was the truth.

"Watch it," barked Schultz. "We aren't taken in by lies, d'you hear? We know perfectly well where you were on the first. Now answer, you sod."

"If you know, why ask me?"

I thought Schultz was going to kill me there and then. He grabbed hold of a pistol, cocked it, and aimed. Then he changed his mind and, nimble as a monkey, unhooked a dog whip from the wall, and lashed out with all his strength at my left temple and eye. It was the eye that Ernst had closed a few hours earlier. I was blinded by a curtain of fire. The pain was so sharp that I keeled over towards the desk, but Ernst caught me before I fell and sent me hurtling into an armchair. The handcuffs cut deeper still into my wrists.

It was then that I experienced a totally new feeling—hatred. I had never felt this before, not even when I was a prisoner of war in Germany. I had heard of brutality. I had even seen Russian political commissars tortured. But human beings are odd creatures, for we only know what it is like when it is our own flesh that is made to suffer. My illusions vanished. I was seized by this new feeling, and coldly resolved never to yield, never to be broken. The guffaw emitted by that Cro-Magnon brute Ernst only made me all the more determined.

"Get up," shouted Schultz. "None of that slouching. Stand here before the desk. Where were you on the first of September?"

Sitting behind a typewriter, he took off his spectacles and looked me over. I stared him out and struggled not to spit in his face. He was not a rat, but a hyena, a vulture, with his bulbous forehead, his broken, yellow teeth with the protruding canines, and his nasty blubber lip.

"I really can't remember. I must have been at Bourbon-l'Archambault with my family."

"Filthy liar. Hypocrite. You were at Châteauroux unloading an English Halifax full of arms. Has that jogged your memory now? Or perhaps it was an American Liberator?"

"Nonsense. I never set foot in Châteauroux. I never heard of—"

"Shut up, you bleeding rat. You'd better confess now, or we'll make you."

Confess—that was the magic word. That was what I was to hear all night long. "Confess!"

The Gestapo were obsessively punctilious about their confessions. They were ready to snuff out your life on the slightest pretext after they had practised on you refinements of torture that would have made the medieval inquisitors turn pale. They had to have formal confessions properly set out, signed, witnessed, initialled, registered, which were then copied and sent out with a statement and inventory to various departments and archives. Once the paperwork was out of their way, they quickly got you out of their way as well.

It did not matter particularly what you confessed to. Their main concern was the accumulation of as many confessions as possible, and the more long-winded, improbable, incredible, outrageously extravagant they were, the more they liked them. They were not sticklers for detail, nor did they sort out the plausible from the impossible. Their credulity, or crass stupidity, was boundless—had I decided to tell them that I had been entrusted with the job of blowing up the Alma bridge in Paris and arming the Resistance with its stones, or that I had swum the Channel in order to fight them, I am sure they would have believed it and taken it down in writing. Schultz and Basedow, with whom I had to contend, would have swallowed it anyway.

The Bourges Gestapo did not enjoy the geographic advantages of, say, the Vercors, the Glières, the Jura, and the Pyrenees ones. The area did not lend itself to maquis operations.

The Gestapo here had only managed to catch small fry, a few railway saboteurs, explosives thieves at the gunpowder factory, a couple of minor agents. There had been no dramatic round-ups. Top Gestapo sleuths probably never set foot in Bourges. They were kept busy round the 'hot spots' of Toulouse, Besançon, Grenoble. The Berry cattle farmers and the vintners round Sancerre were a very wily lot. The German police were up against an alert, well-organized group which threw up an impenetrable wall of silence. They had a few informers but they were usually short-changed.

The headquarters at Paris, Oberg, and Knochen were not satisfied. They bombarded the rue Michel-de-Bourges with all manner of questionnaires and statistics, and hustled and bullied Hasse the whole time. "What the devil do you think you're doing? You have not come up with a terrorist, with a saboteur, or even a spy in your area. You're all taking it far too easy and lazing around in the sunshine getting fat. This is just not good enough."

Then Hasse and his underlings would put on a great show of energy. They would arrest anyone and everyone they could possibly lay hands on. They took hostages. They sent dossiers stuffed full of confessions to Paris. And it was all done for promotion—promotion and cash bonuses were the incentives. The bonuses were arranged on a sliding scale: so much for a terrorist, so much for a spy, so much for a parachutist.

This explains why Franz Schultz was tired of the singularly unrewarding task of interrogating crafty local farmers. It also explains why we got the reception we did. We were something of a scoop, a real windfall. He would capitalize on the case and blow it up out of all proportion. Yves and I became important leaders of a dangerous network. We had been sent on a special mission by de Gaulle himself. We had become every policeman's dream come true—we would make his career, he would be promoted, and he could then wear an extra piece of braid. He would be one up on a couple of colleagues he hated: Kurt Reidel, a Magdeburg accountant, and Max Winterling, a Breslau engineer. They were paltry amateurs by comparison to him, for he thought of himself as a veritable Sherlock Holmes.

Unfortunately, my stubborn refusal to confess upset his plans and frustrated his dreams. "Are you or aren't you going to confess and tell us what you were really doing on the first? Do you want to be persuaded some more? We could plug some electric wires into your testicles, for a start. That can be quite unpleasant."

"I can't tell you what I don't know."

"All right. You've asked for it!"

He was so furious that his thick German accent took over, and his two favourite French oaths, "canaille" (scum) and "crapule" (filthy swine), became "ganaille" and "grabule".

He nodded to Basedow and said in German, "Get the dog out of here."

This was the moment our flaxen giant had been waiting for. He almost started licking his lips in anticipation.

I had not noticed the dog. He came out from beneath the table, a magnificent black and tan Alsatian with a fine, glossy coat. He sniffed at me as he passed and I thought I detected an almost human look in his eye, so accustomed had I become to Ernst's bestial expression—Ernst, the huge, eighteen-stone animal, all muscle and fat, and always reeking of old cigars and stale beer.

Ernst went to a cupboard and brought out a flexible rubber tube filled with lead. It was about two fingers thick and three feet long. He removed his jacket, rolled up his shirt sleeves, and threw out his chest. He stood squarely, feet apart, trousers bursting over his enormous hams, hose in hand, smiling benignly, and said to me in German, "All set. Now for some fun."

"Turn round," said Schultz. "Let's have your back."

This was it. This was the moment of truth. I was determined to show them I was a man. I felt strong and resolute.

[40]

Ernst delivered the first blow with all his strength. It walloped down viciously on my shoulder blades. I stood my ground, gritted my teeth, and steeled myself for the second. This one came down on my handcuffed hands behind my back. That really hurt. The third cut into my buttocks and kidneys and reverberated in my belly.

Schultz started up his monotonous litany once again. "Where were you on the first, you filthy swine?"

I had no time to reply. Schultz and Basedow were not well co-ordinated. Down came the fourth blow on to the backs of my knees. Ernst was getting into full swing. He was in his element, and started lashing out all over the place at a tremendous speed. I forced myself to get used to it. I stifled screams and kept telling myself that one ought to be able to hold out against torture. I forced myself to think of other things. I imagined I was outside my body, somewhere else, on the Côte d'Azur I loved so much and would probably never see again.

"Wait a minute, Ernst. We won't get anywhere like this. Take off his jacket and shirt and bring his arms forward."

This gave me a small but very welcome rest.

While Basedow ripped off my clothes to save time, Schultz preached on. "Why won't you be reasonable? Come on. Sign the statement. It's all ready for you. Then we'll leave you alone. Your brother was much more co-operative, you know. He told us everything. We know there's a nest of spies at Bourbon-l'Archambault, and we know about your uncle and your cousin. We even know who you are working for. Come on, do as your brother did. Confess. Perhaps I should tell you that your brother voluntarily made a clean breast of the whole thing. We didn't lay a finger on him once."

I was not taken in.

"Just as you're not laying a finger on me, I suppose?"

Schultz was very touchy, and resented my doubting his word. He really had the idea that he was some sort of super brain, with what he thought was the air of a bespectacled, astute intellectual, whereas in fact his trick questions were unworthy of a ten-year-old and about as obvious as a poppy in a cornfield. They were a grotesque pair: numbskull Basedow with his buffalo body and puny little Schultz with his guilty, perjurer's face. They seemed to be hand in glove but they were probably madly jealous of each other. They, like all the other thirteen Gestapo agents at Bourges, fought lethal silent battles for supremacy. They were all ex-gaolbirds, layabouts, thugs, and hooligans, fresh from the Lübeck or Hamburg underworlds. Their only real bond was a mutual lust for pleasure and power.

Recruitment must have been a problem for Himmler. He had to find staff to do this sort of work all over occupied Europe from Narvik to Catania, from Biarritz to Odessa. The head of the Reich Police had solved the personnel problem by looking appropriately to his unemployed criminals, for these he could control with constant blackmail. There was no room for recalcitrants in the new order, and the system ensured that these recruits would work themselves to death to curry favour.

Schultz was becoming almost hysterically furious.

"Here, hold his wrists. I'll show him!"

Basedow held my arms in a vice-like grip, bent me forward, put my hands flat on the desk, and belched vilely in my face. He smelt of sweat and old leather.

A battery of strokes from a metal ruler hammered down on my fingernails. The harder Schultz struck, the wilder he became. He was obviously a genuine sadist yielding to his more savage impulses. Perhaps his ugliness had caused his complexes, or perhaps I suddenly became an expiatory whipping boy for all his failings, for his mediocrity. Some disturbed people find real sexual satisfaction in doing violence to a man reduced to their mercy, and Schultz was probably this sort of pervert. I screamed and wriggled, but Basedow held me down. The handcuffs bit into my wrists, and beads of blood sprang from my fingertips, leaving red fingerprints on the desk top. Basedow locked me between his wrestler's thighs.

Unused to such exercise, Schultz tired and stopped. "That'll teach you," he panted. "I won't be made a fool of. We've been too nice to you. We'll string you up like we strung your blasted brother. Let him have it, Ernst."

What did he mean? Had they hanged Yves? Surely not.

I only found out later that they had actually strung him up to make him talk, and then cut him down at the last moment.

[42]

The battering started up again, punctuated with Schultz monotonously harping "Where were you on the first? Confess, damn you, confess."

My back, chest, knees, ribs, shins, and face all received a beating. Basedow wielded the pipe as a woodcutter his axe. His shirt was soaking wet and he was breathing heavily, but he kept on and on. All I could do was yell. The pain came from everywhere. I was in agony.

Ernst was getting tired. The leaded pipe was losing impetus.

"Go on, go on," urged Schultz. "He's almost ready."

"Das hat keinen Wert ["there's no point"]," gasped Ernst.

I then made a terrible mistake. I said to Schultz, in German, "Nein, das hat keinen Wert."

They gaped at me speechless.

"So you can speak German can you, you filthy swine? You were hiding that, eh? I've had to wear myself out speaking French while you know German. Why the bloody hell didn't you tell us?"

"You never asked. You questioned me in French and I answered in French. Had I answered in German you would have found fault with that too."

"Take that," roared Schultz.

The dog leash whipped across my face twice, ripping a gash from ear to mouth.

I lost control of myself then, which only made matters worse, and I let him have it in German. "You pig, you lousy, lowdown Kraut. You know damn' well that if we were fighting man to man I'd have ground you to a pulp long ago."

Strangely enough he did not seem to take great exception to this, but simply turned to Basedow and said, "Carry on, Ernst."

"I've had enough. Get one of the others. It's about time they did something."

Two criminal-looking thugs came to take over. "Mind the dog," Ernst shouted. "Shut the door."

The Alsatian had been scratching and whining and barking at the door all during the session. He had been trained, after all, to be in at the kill.

[43]

"Get on with it, Peter," said Schultz.

Peter had the same sort of build as Ernst, and probably specialized in the same sort of exertion.

"Know what the Berlin spinning top is?" he said, in bad French.

"You can talk German to that pig, he understands."

Peter Emmerich let down from the ceiling a double chain on a pulley, the kind mechanics use in garages for hauling up car engines. He undid my handcuffs and twisted my hands into them behind my back. He then attached the chain between the handcuffs to a hook that hung from the tackle, and pulled on the chain. I was thus hauled up by the hands, but the strain fell mostly on my shoulders. I hung with my arms pulled up behind me, my feet a couple of feet above the floor. I could either tip forward completely or make an enormous effort to straighten up, and when I tried doing that the object of the contraption became clear. The top part of my back and the muscles of my chest contracted under the strain of remaining upright and finally locked solid in an agonizing spasm. The pain in my wrists was unbearable. But if the setting-up was excruciating it was nothing compared with what was to come. Emmerich and the other gorilla both grabbed a leaded pipe and thumped away at me as I hung there like a broken puppet. I began to turn at the end of the chain with the impact of their vicious blows. Blood spurted all over the place. I had blood in my eyes and blood trickled down my trousers. I was isolated in a world of blows that came alternately from the two henchmen. I turned and spun like a top. I could no longer see; a purple haze hovered about my head, and I was only just conscious enough to hear Schultz's shrill voice repeating over and over again, "Confess, you terrorist, you spy, confess and we'll stop."

I mustered up the last of my strength to yell out in French, "Murderers, cowards, bastards, kill me. Come on, why don't you kill me?"

But gradually and inexorably my willpower was dwindling away. I kept trying to get a grip on myself, to hold on, but I could not. The torn muscles in my arms and torso were literally killing me. I was on the verge of confessing. I knew now what it was to be tortured and how it conditions one psychologically.

[44]

If Yves had been through this I understood how he would have confessed to anything they wanted.

To confess . . . To put an end to my miseries . . . To stop the pain in the back of my neck . . .

Torture is an easy and quick way out for incompetent policemen anxious to get some sort of result. It is the Roman *argumentum baculinum* (arguing with a stick) which Molière's Sganarelle uses in *Le Mariage Forcé*. It is a quick solution for dimwits of low mental ability. A good detective who knows his stuff can always make a suspect give himself away or contradict himself during a skilfully conducted interrogation. However, that takes patience and intelligence and Schultz certainly did not possess either. Torture has its cracking point. Everyone who does not possess vast mental and moral reserves eventually cracks. Not everyone can be a Jean Moulin[1] or Pierre Brossolette.[2] I was not broken by drugs, blackmail, or psychological torture. My spirit was not broken but my body was, by the constant battery of blows pounding the same extra-sensitive parts: groin, knees, hands, thighs, face.

I think it was Drieu La Rochelle who wrote: "Stand your ground, stick to the truth until they strike you down. Don't run off . . ."

I would like to have seen Drieu La Rochelle in my shoes. The more I stuck to the truth the harder they struck me down. I should have liked nothing better than to run off, but the Gestapo would obviously have none of that.

I think the Nazis also used torture to punish and vilify the "criminals, bandits, gangsters, and terrorists", as they qualified those who dared oppose them. The posters they stuck all over Paris announcing the execution of patriots did their best to discredit them in the eyes of their fellow-countrymen—they even did this to irreproachable heroes like Estienne d'Orves[3] the Free French naval officer.

In one last moment of lucidity, when I thought I would crack and confess, I told myself I had to find some sort of dodge that would put a stop to all this—and suddenly it came of its own accord. My stomach muscles contracted violently, and I retched and spewed up all over Schultz at my side.

[1] See Translators' Notes, p. 173.　[2] *Ibid.*, p. 173.　[3] *Ibid.*, p. 174.

That put a stop to the Berlin top.

"You filthy bleeding pig," spluttered Schultz. "You'll pay for that."

Ernst let down the tackle and I collapsed onto the floor. Schultz, covered in vomit, kicked me up and dragged me by the scruff of the neck into the lavatory. He rammed my head down the lavatory bowl while someone else pulled the chain. This was Schultz's refinement of the bath torture. I choked and swallowed the lavatory water stained with my own blood. It went up my nose. I tried to breathe but got a lung full of water instead. I nearly drowned three times and three times Schultz pulled me out and pushed me back in again leaning heavily on my neck. He never let up his infernal chant, "Where were you on the first? Are you going to talk, or do you want us to rip off your fingernails?"

All I could do was to cry feebly for help.

Schultz put a stop to my cries with another of his flashes of ingenuity. He stuffed the dog's blanket, covered in hairs, down my throat. I coughed and was choking to death. I gasped desperately for breath. The dog's hairs stuck to the back of my throat. Schultz kept bellowing, "Confess. Where were you on the first? Come on, confess."

In the end Basedow had to interrupt.

"That's enough, Fritz. Don't let him die. I'm sure he wants to."

Schultz cooled down a bit. He dismissed the other two bruisers with a curt, "Thanks for your help. We won't be needing you any more. Ernst and I can manage now."

Emmerich, the nastier of the two, kicked me in the stomach as he passed. "See you at the firing range. Perhaps you won't be so cocky then."

It was on the Bourges firing range that the condemned prisoners faced the firing squad.

Ernst pushed me into the armchair where I collapsed.

The door opened and a sinister-looking man appeared holding a dog on a leash. He was wearing a black leather jacket that was too short for him over baggy jodhpurs and boots, and held a riding crop in his left hand. He was dark and swarthy with cruel green eyes.

[46]

"Here's our friend Paoli.[1] He's a fellow countryman of yours, you know," said Schultz waggishly. "He's our nail-ripping specialist. Paoli, why don't you try your hand at our friend here who won't talk? I'm sure you could persuade him." Here we were in the middle of the twentieth century and in walks a nail-ripping specialist from the days of General Valdès, the Inquisitor General. And he was Corsican, a fellow-countryman of Bonaparte no less. I could not believe it. I nearly wept with shame.

Paoli turned towards me slowly and stared. I don't know whether he reacted to the scorn I had in my eyes, but he hesitated a moment, then said in German, "No, I'm busy. I've got to go up to the prison to see a Jew the police have sent us from Vierzon."

"Oh, well," said Schultz, and then turned to me and said, "You can thank your lucky stars." He replaced the pincers, jack-knife, and screwdriver he had taken out of the drawer for Paoli.

"Well, now, let's have a little chat," said Schultz. "I think you are going to be a little more co-operative now. Ever seen this before?"

I recognized Yves's diary.

"On August 27th it says, 'Three rolls from Pinel's.' They weren't rolls of gelignite, by any chance?"

I found it hard to speak. My jaws were locked, my nose bled, and I kept bringing up lavatory water.

"Pinel is a baker at Bourbon-l'Archambault. My brother must have gone shopping on August 27th and bought some bread."

"Pinel is a Resistance leader in the Allier. Your brother told us so."

In any other circumstances the idea of poor old Pinel being a Resistance leader would have struck me as hilariously funny. I could not imagine Pinel hiding away gelignite and surreptitiously passing information over the counter.

"My brother couldn't possibly have told you that. Pinel is a quiet little tradesman."

"It's precisely the quiet ones who shoot us in the back in this

[1] See Appendices, p. 171.

[47]

bloody awful country. So you know nothing about this baker, then? All right, we'll arrest him and bring you two face to face. What about this Jean Doyen? Where did your brother go to meet him? What role did he play in your organization?"

"Jean Doyen? Never heard of him."

"What's that, then?"

He pointed to where Yves had written under May 20th, "Jean Doyen concert."

"Oh, yes. He's a pianist my brother went to hear in Paris."

"Pianist my arse. He's a terrorist leader. Your brother told us so."

Had my poor brother gone quite out of his mind to implicate everyone and accuse them all wrongly? I understood how he might have done so if he had undergone the kind of treatment they had just handed out to me.

"What about the Prefect, the Allier Prefect. He's your chief, isn't he? Or are you the Gaullist leader?"

"How does the Prefect come into it?"

"Don't you come the innocent with me. You know damn' well what I mean, and so does your brother. I think our friend Ernst might have to refresh your memory a bit. What about it, Ernst?"

"Jawohl!" answered the giant.

I shuddered at the thought of standing up to any more. I could not take it. I had been sitting crouched in the armchair with my hands behind my back, and I was shivering. My chest was still bare and bleeding. I dared not lean against the chair back because of my wounds. I would never be able to get up by myself—they would have to carry me.

"Get this into your thick French skull, you pig—Basedow here has only patted you about so far. He has all sorts of things tucked up his sleeve. He's a strong fellow and very resourceful. Let's talk about you a bit. What did you come here to do? Who were you supposed to meet in Bourges?"

"I've already told your lady interpreter all about it."

"Shut up about Annie, she's just the boss's girl, nothing more."

"I came here confident that I'd get news of my brother. If I had anything to conceal from you lot, I'd scarcely have come knocking at your door."

[48]

Then Schultz came out with a classic remark which spoke volumes for his degree of intelligence: "We all know that the greatest criminals return to the scene of their crime."

I had a fever. My teeth were chattering, my head spun, and I saw everything through a haze. Schultz noticed the state I was in.

"What about a cup of coffee and a cigarette? Take his handcuffs off, Ernst, and let him dress."

My hands were numb, purple and icy. As I looked at them it suddenly occurred to me that I would never be able to play tennis again, which just goes to show what a state I was in.

Ernst put on the remains of my tattered shirt, and Schultz brought me the coffee. I had no time to drink it, however. The menace that had hung in the air since our departure from the barber's shop that morning suddenly became a reality. The door opened and the very same Gestapo agent we had seen strode in. Hermann Yeske was even viler than we had thought. I know one is not entirely to blame for one's physical endowments, but this man could never have been anything other than what he was. One could not imagine him as, say, a florist, a head waiter, a musician. He could only be a torturer. He was an executioner straight from the time of François Villon, the kind that used to hold axed heads aloft for public inspection at the Place de Grève in 1450, that strung up the condemned on the Montfaucon gallows.

Yeske stopped in the doorway and looked surprised to see me. Rigid as a statue, he pointed to me and exclaimed, "But I know this one. I saw him at the barber's this morning with an arrogant bastard who insulted me."

Schultz and Ernst were amazed.

Before I could take hold of myself, Schultz's whip caught my right hand and spilt the coffee over my lap.

"His name was Delescure, wasn't it?" he barked.

I was caught off my guard. My mind had seized up and my reactions were dull. I agreed. Claude and I would pay dearly for our rashness.

A bunch of real bruisers including Hasse pounced on me and shook the daylights out of me.

"Where is he? What was he doing? Where's he gone?"

They were shouting like lunatics. Schultz kept yelling shrilly,
"Fooled us again, eh? You shit. You'll tell us where he is or I'll
wring your bloody neck."

He was in such a frenzy that I really thought he would. I had
to save Claude come what may. For Schultz it was his promotion that was at stake. For Claude, Yves, and myself it was our
lives.

"He's taking the train to Paris where he'll hide."

I knew perfectly well that Claude would leave Bourges that
evening for Bourbon-l'Archambault.

Hermann Yeske shouted, "We've got time. The train leaves
Bourges at ten past midnight. It's five to now. Come on, all out
to the station and we'll get him."

They all rushed off like hounds to the kill. Hasse, their boss,
shouted after them, "Turn the train inside out. Delay it if
necessary, but bring him back dead or alive. If need be two of
you stay on the train as far as Paris, but don't let him get away.
My God, we'll have some fun. Yeske, you're in charge. We'll
have the whole lot. All we need is Delescure and the uncle."

"Yes, sir," said Yeske, "it will be my pleasure. I've a personal
score to settle with him, and I'll see to it myself as soon as we get
back. In the meantime, my friend, take that for this morning's
little episode."

He gave me two resounding blows across my face with the
back of his hand, which merely added to what I had already
had.

They sprang into action, rattling weapons, barking orders,
clanging down the stairs and revving up their engines. I remained
with my two delectable companions, Basedow and Schultz.

"See what you're like? There we were trusting you, and all
you do is repay us with lies! Why didn't you tell us your cousin
was in Bourges? You've been wasting our time, haven't you, and
now we'll have to start again from scratch. You've been with us
for two hours and we haven't got anywhere. All this pride
doesn't do you any good, does it? We'll go over your cousin a bit
before your very eyes, and he'll tell us everything. Well, now.
Why was your cousin in Bourges? Was he also worried about
your brother? You must take us for a bunch of fools, but this
nonsense has gone far enough."

[50]

I was at the end of my tether, exhausted, dazed, and thirsty. My mouth was swollen and sticky with blood. As my plight could not be much worse, I became reckless and gave bent to my last reserves of anger. I let fly in French, "You bastards! You can bloody well ask my cousin what he was up to when you've got him. Go to hell. You don't believe a thing I say; so go to hell and be damned."

It actually worked. I was amazed. "All right, all right. We'll get at Delescure soon enough. And you'd better see to it that your stories tally or you'll both be for it. Now tell us about yourself."

He sat down at his typewriter and took down a statement. The text was entirely his own and had been prepared beforehand. He knew all about my family, my brothers, cousin, uncle, my 1940 campaign. The family file was complete and correct. Yves must have been voluble under torture. I answered in monosyllables. I agreed with the positive facts he gave me, but I held out against my supposed complicity in the Resistance in the Cher, and insisted it was a fantasy of theirs. I knew that if I signed I would be writing my own death warrant. Schultz alternated between menaces and pleas. He called me selfish. He threatened to arrest my family. He made insidious comparisons between me and my brother in a prim, moralizing tone which suited him about as well as a lace bonnet would a cow. If Schultz had known that I had almost confessed everything an hour ago he would have gone mad. Had I yielded then, I would be a condemned man awaiting sure death.

Ernst, temporarily relieved of his distinguished services, swung around the room like a caged bear. Every now and then he would stop to fling a few insults in my face and threaten me with one of his flashes of inspiration. This finally got on Schultz's nerves.

"For Christ's sake, shut up. I can't concentrate. Have a beer or something."

He took a swig, belched, scratched himself, and started swinging around again.

Three-quarters of an hour later, the others returned. My two hounds leered with anticipation.

My heart almost stopped beating. What if Claude had

changed his mind and really taken the Paris train? If he had, we could only pray for a Christian burial, all three of us.

The door flung open. Hermann blew in and made straight for me, lifted me out of the chair, and bawled, "Lousy bastard. So you thought you could pull a fast one on us, did you? Your cousin's escaped, but you'll get his dose."

There were a good ten of them in the room, all armed to the teeth, arguing and gesticulating in their disappointment.

"We searched every inch of the train and there wasn't a trace of him. We held it up for half an hour. He just wasn't on it," shouted Hermann.

Then Hermann beat the daylights out of me with the hose. The thrashing was in the best sadistic tradition. He laid into me with savage, destructive violence. He gripped the hose with both hands and swung downwards like a slaughterman hammering cattle to death, aiming at my knees. Time and again I was convinced he'd cracked my fibula and that my kneecaps were bursting. But, without boasting, dear cousin, who shared my childhood, who won honours at Dien Bien Phu yet never lost your simplicity, I can honestly say that I accepted my hiding in your place with real joy because it meant you had escaped those killers and that you were free.

Hermann's fury finally abated. He turned his wrath onto Schultz, his SS equal. He called him a good-for-nothing, a third-rate ham, a measly little failure. Schultz returned the compliments roundly. I never realized German had such a marvellous vocabulary of abuse. Just like the Arabs, they held the other's mother responsible for their offsprings' vices. They thrashed each other verbally. Had Schultz been in better trim he would have settled his score with the hose. It was like two wolves fighting.

Meanwhile, the remainder of the pack hung about, quite impassive, waiting to take sides, to see who would come out the winner.

Hermann finally broke off in disgust. "You wanted to handle this. Well, you're up to your neck in it now. Try wriggling out of this one. You really know what you're doing, don't you? You've let the real criminal get right through your fingers. You're nothing but an incompetent fool."

[52]

He stalked out, nose in the air, followed by Basedow.

I was left alone with Schultz, and had a feeling I would have to pay dearly for the duel.

"Well now, I've got a little surprise in store for you. Since you won't tell us the truth, we're going to bring you face to face with you know who. One of you will have to spill the beans."

I could not believe that the thing I saw entering was Yves. He came in on a leash, led by Basedow. Was this wreck of a man with a vacant, hang-dog expression, who stumbled about like a robot, really my happy, energetic brother I had last seen twelve short days ago? He was an appalling sight. Even his eyes had changed. They had that haunted, panic-stricken look of a hunted animal. I dreaded to think what they must have done to him to change him beyond all recognition. One side of his face was swollen, one of his eyebrows gashed open, and clots of dried blood blotched his forehead. He was filthy and ragged, and could not stand up properly.

He did not recognize me immediately. He just stood there, exhausted and lost. Basedow and Schultz sneered idiotically.

"Well now, my young terrorist brothers," said Ernst, "we want to know which of you has been lying."

Tears came to my eyes when I thought of the hell Yves must have been through and when I saw his left arm, partially paralysed by his 1940 wound, clamped into handcuffs.

Suddenly something seemed to click and he came to his senses a little.

"Oh, it's you, Marc," he muttered. "What are you doing here? They've let you have it too, I see."

"Shut up, you two. There'll be no talking between you. I'm asking the questions," howled Schultz.

"Now you, the tall one," he said to me, "are you going to go on telling me that you have nothing to do with the Resistance, that you've done nothing, and that all you wanted to do was 'rescue' your brother?"

"Yes."

He turned to Yves. "And what about you, you louse? Do you still maintain that your brother here was the commander-in-chief of the Resistance, that he went to Châteauroux on September 1st with Pinel, Jean Doyen, Degrave, and all the others?"

"It's not true," cried Yves. "I never said that."

"You didn't, eh?" Schultz rapped out. "Well, what's this, then? It's all down here in your statement which you've signed."

"I wasn't in my right mind. I didn't know what I was signing."

"Pig, you can't wriggle out of it just like that. Why don't you admit you were trying to save your own skin by putting the blame on everyone else including your brother here? You're a revolting little skunk and a bloody liar as well. How could you do such a thing to a brother? It's nauseating. Your brother is here because you betrayed him. It's all your fault."

Schultz was quite loathsome. He was trying to pit us against each other. He put on all sorts of altruistic airs and adopted the charitable tone of a defender of widows and orphans. He knew perfectly well that Yves had lost his reason because they had kicked his head in. He may also have been warped and stupid enough to think he could take me in with his childish tactics.

He was really playing up to me. "See what a brother you've got. He's given us a different story every day. He's made a fool of us. We believed him. He's done everything he could think of to put all the blame on your shoulders. Your brother's a nasty bit of work, a nasty little liar!"

Even though I knew I would not get away with it, I decided to speak up, and told him what I thought of his ploy. "If you hadn't beaten him senseless he wouldn't have given you all that rubbish."

"Shut up. Don't shoot your damn' mouth off about things you know nothing about. You'll go down into a nice little cell while we straighten out your brother's lies."

An SS guard came to drag me off. I managed to whisper to Yves, "Good luck, old boy. Don't let them get the better of you."

He gave me a terribly pathetic look. He probably thought I held him responsible and resented him for it, and I found this more difficult to bear than the beatings.

I was put into a special cell. It was a narrow, vertical coffin which might almost have been made to measure. It was about six feet high and fitted so closely that when the door closed I felt it against me. I could not move an inch, and my hands were tied behind my back. I was surprised to find a small door oppo-

site my face: what could it be for? I was in the coal-cellar again
and in total darkness.

My back, legs, and face were in great pain. I could not rest
as I was held upright by the narrowness of the cupboard. The
only way I could breathe was to lean against the little door. I
heard heavy thumping sounds from above, though there were no
ensuing cries. It was Yves being beaten by that frantic brute
Basedow.

Yves was paying for Claude's escape. Schultz, Basedow, and
Yeske took Claude's safety as a personal insult.

The flogging went on for over half an hour. Every thud reverberated through the floor joists and boards into my very bones.

The cellar light switched on and Basedow and Schultz
appeared.

"We're going to treat you to a 'Son et Lumière' show,"
chuckled Schultz.

He brought forward something fixed on a tripod and set it up
a foot or so from my face in the little doorway. It was a large
reflector bowl which gaped darkly before me, one of those anti-
aircraft searchlight reflectors that penetrates clouds several
thousand feet up. Schultz pressed a switch and a million suns burst
into my cubbyhole and shot through my eyes, drilling fiercely
into my skull. My brain contracted and prickled with a million
white-hot needles. My retinas burnt, my pupils dilated and paralysed. This, then, was Hell itself, the fires of damnation. I tried
to escape the searing beam by turning my head and squeezing
my eyes shut, but eyelids were no protection against such white
heat. They started crackling like burnt paper. The back of my
neck started sizzling. I was stifling. I panicked and tried to
struggle but the fire held me in its grip. I was slipping and sliding farther and farther into Hell, and eventually I fainted.

I came round when Schultz threw a bucket of water over me
through the doorway. Trial by fire and water. I was soaking wet,
and floundered in the water that rose in the cupboard. Everything swam before my eyes, which were full of large, yellow
saucers of light. My neck was still burning. Basedow pulled me
out, and to ensure that I had really come to he clouted me in the
face for the last time. Upstairs I found Yves. He was still groggy
from his beating with the hose.

[55]

We were bundled into a black Citroën, handcuffed to each other, me with my hands behind my back, Yves had his before him because of his crippled arm. Basedow sat up next to the driver with a gun in his hand. Schultz and Riedel sat in the back. Yves risked asking me, "Did they get you at Bourbon?"

A sharp "Ruhe" cut him short.

"One more peep out of you and I'll bust your face in," said Ernst.

It must have been about two o'clock in the morning when we arrived at the Bordiot prison. It stood on a hill between the station and the cemetery. Schultz put on his witty voice and cracked one of his feeble, vicious jokes to Yves. "You arrive on the left by train and leave on the right to the cemetery."

The prison warders had to dig us out of the car and heave us out like a couple of sacks of flour. I was all in and Yves was no better. I heard Schultz warmly introducing us to the German prison staff.

"They're dangerous terrorists and need to be watched day and night. Keep the tall, brazen chap in solitary and put the younger one into a dark cell for a couple of weeks. Bread and water every three days. Give us a buzz if anything happens. Beat them up if they're any trouble."

Two German NCOs lifted me into Cell 67 on the second floor. Yves managed to drag himself along and he disappeared downstairs. I was locked up. It was pitch dark, but I could still see the bright, yellow saucers dancing before my eyes. I was afraid I was going to lose my eyesight. My hands were still shackled.

I was still lucid enough to start assessing the consequences of my mad attempt to rescue Yves.

Why had I risked such a thing? Why? Why? I had not simply rushed into it rashly. I had *known* all along I would be caught. I had sensed it before I even knew what I was going to do. I had even put on an old suit and good tough shoes before leaving Bourbon. I must have known I was going to spend that night in prison.

When I rang the bell at the Gestapo headquarters I overestimated my capabilities and strength. I was over-confident and utterly ignorant of the enemy's methods. But I believed in my mission. I was the elder brother and I felt responsible. Then

[56]

again, Yves had done something in 1940. He had seen action. He had been wounded, whereas I had done nothing. I may have wanted to do my bit to restore the balance.

I lay all trussed up on my pallet turning over the whys and wherefores of the situation.

Our prospects were not exactly promising but then they could not get worse. Yves seemed to have regained his wits. Claude was free. Even if I hadn't convinced Schultz, I had not confessed. My continued existence was still hanging by a very slender thread and the immediate future was anything but rosy. But Yves, I am afraid, was much worse off.

[IV]

Claude waited for me in the café in Bourges where I had left him. He did not think there was any great likelihood that I would rejoin him. He gave me an extra half-hour and hung about until half-past five. Then it occurred to him that if they succeeded in making me talk they would know of our meeting place, so he left and went into the first restaurant he came across in order to get off the streets. This was in the rue Auron and the owner, Guittard, happened to be connected with the Berry Resistance. Claude cautiously told him in very general terms what had happened and asked him to take a food parcel to his cousins in prison. The man did so.

He advised Claude to get to the station before midnight when the curfew started, and to hide in a goods wagon and await the arrival of the Moulins train. Claude burrowed under a pile of skins, between crates of sanitary goods and sheets of corrugated iron which were on their way to the occupying forces' outposts. This hiding place saved him. He heard the commotion the Gestapo made when they searched the Paris train for him.

When the pack had given up the chase he calmly climbed out, found a seat on the passenger train bound for Bourbon-l'Archambault, and got home without more ado.

Uncle Frédéric—we called him Uncle Freddy—took the dreadful news calmly.

"The first thing we must do is see to the equipment. Claude, you will have to try to make it to Switzerland to warn your chiefs."[1]

Uncle Freddy was at the time harbouring several Resistance men, secret agents, and labour-camp dodgers. One of them was Francis, a sort of reluctant resister. He had been allotted the task

[1] Claude's information was transmitted to Allied Intelligence in Switzerland.

that Yves had finally carried out. Francis had got cold feet or had been too lazy to go, and was therefore indirectly responsible for Yves's arrest, as Yves had had to stand in for him at the last moment. Uncle Freddy asked him to pitch his tent elsewhere. Then there was a Polish officer from the Anders army. He was always convinced that D-Day was just around the corner, so they had to find him another hideout in the area. Every trace of these unusual guests' presence had to be eradicated. Then the family settled down to make themselves ready for the onslaught of the German police.

Claude did not try getting to Switzerland his usual way through Mornet and Annemasse where he was assured a safe crossing, but took the precaution of going through the wild Jura mountains. Not without difficulty he reached a tavern in a village in the Orbe valley from where he phoned his chiefs in Berne, then went on to the Swiss capital to meet his chief, General W. He was a perfect example of the kind of English officer that André Maurois described in *Les Silences du Colonel Bramble*, and was the head of British Intelligence in Switzerland.

Claude soon got to the point. "My last mission went wrong, very wrong. My two cousins are under arrest and I am implicated. I have come to ask your help. We must try to get my cousins out. Could the RAF—"

General W. cut him short. "I'm sorry. His Majesty's Services have their rules and we stick to them except in very extraordinary circumstances. We consider an agent captured as an agent lost. We've got agents all over occupied Europe, not to mention the Middle East. We just can't lay on a full-scale rescue operation every time one of them is caught, however much we might like to. Why not rustle up something in the area, get the local FFI[1] to help?"

"I'd thought of that. But it's impossible."

"It must be terrible for you, and I do hope you will believe that I fully sympathize with your family's distress. But please don't ask me to help you. I cannot make exceptions. Your work must go on. I have things for you to do."

He told Claude to go to Évreux in Normandy, where the German airfields were crammed full of planes. But the General's

[1] See Translators' Notes, p. 173.

refusal to help dampened Claude's enthusiasm. The old fervour, the loyalty and magic of it all, had disappeared. He left Berne a disillusioned man. General W. had told him where he could cross the frontier. He went to Montluçon and phoned a friend of the family, Madame Guyard, in Bourbon-l'Archambault.

"Oh, hello, Claude. Well Uncle Jules,[1] the one you don't like and who doesn't like you either, wants to get in touch with you. He's angry with you and he's taken Uncle Freddy with him to his place at Vichy to . . . to make him contact you."

"Yes, I see. Well, thanks." And Claude hung up. Well, that did it. General W. and the British could stuff their damn' missions. He set off for his father's house in Paris and went into hiding.

The German police had finally turned up at Uncle Freddy's. They had taken their time. At the crack of dawn on September 19th, four solid-looking specimens dressed to the eyebrows in long, grey, imitation-leather raincoats, despite the heat, sprung up in his garden. They clicked their heels and nodded under their nasty green hats, which they wore squashed over their ears. They were always conspicuously the same: stereotyped Kraut cops that might have stepped out of a second-feature spy film.

Our little twenty-year-old maid Marie from Ygrande saw them rush into the garden as if they were on manœuvres. She had the presence of mind to rush round gathering up the photographs of Claude that lay about and shoving them into her apron pocket.

"Madame, madame, they're here," she shouted through the house to wake them all up. "Monsieur Passy, they've come."

In the meantime the policemen were tapping at the french windows overlooking the garden, their revolvers drawn. Marie kept them hanging about as long as she could and then she opened the door, looking as stupid as possible.

"Can I help you, gentlemen?"

"German police. Where's Delescure? Come on. Where's the terrorist? Where's the spy? Out with it," they all bellowed at once, and then pushed her aside and spread through the house like a plague.

---

[1] "Uncle Jules" was our private code word for the Germans.

My uncle decided to show them just how unimpressed he was by all this unnecessary fuss. He came out to greet them in his underpants, holding a shaving brush and his face covered with lather.

"Where's Delescure? Where's that nephew of yours?" they shouted.

"Gentlemen, would you mind not making such a noise? And do put your guns away. You are in my house, and you have my permission to remove your hats and take a seat. We can then discuss this matter in a civilized way."

This haughty, self-possessed educated English type who stood before them unruffled, unperturbed—even in his underpants— and who spoke to them in crisp German, took the wind out of their sails. But they kept their hats firmly squashed on their heads.

"First, you can tell us where your nephew is hiding," said their leader.

"I have no idea. I haven't seen him for days."

"We'll catch him, so you'd better watch out if you've been lying."

They began to search the house, though 'search' was not really the right word. They went through the place like a typhoon. They kicked the furniture over, and ripped it open with chisels. To save time they forced open all the locks they came across with screwdrivers and threw the contents on the floor. Vases of flowers were spilt over the carpets, curtains were ripped down, parquet flooring pulled up, and so on. Aunt Andrée, who had buried herself under the bedclothes in her fear, was made to go down and witness their wanton violence.

Fortunately, my nineteen-year-old cousin Chantal had gone to Paris that day. Had she been at home they would probably have used her to blackmail her parents into confessing and then taken her off as a hostage. It was all the more fortunate since Chantal had been directly involved in conspiring against the Germans. She had been a courier for her father, and used to cycle over the demarcation line with forged papers for the Resistance and with platinum ingots stuffed into the extension tube of her bicycle saddle or into the parson's nose of some plucked chicken or duck. She was plucky and youthfully brazen, and

[61]

could get away with it all because of her blarney and stunning complexion. The German police never suspected this lovely girl in shorts who regularly sailed past their control point at the Madeleine.

The search party suddenly stopped short before a photograph of Chantal astride a powerful motorbike. "Who's this?"

"My daughter Chantal."

"Why the motorbike? Very suspicious."

"She's speed mad. She's always wanted to have a man's motorbike."

"I don't believe you. Motorbikes mean terrorists. Who does the motorbike belong to?"

"I don't know. A friend of hers took the snapshot. Neither of them knew who it belonged to. It just happened to be there and—"

"Ach so! It just happened to be there. We're not fools, not babies, you know. Who is the owner, eh?"

"I really don't know. I've no idea."

"Right. We'll find the gangster who owns it and arrest him. We'll make him talk," they sneered.

The photograph was a close-up and the registration number was perfectly clear, but nonetheless they scrutinized it with a magnifying glass.[1]

The photograph really excited them, and they set to work on the furniture again. One pasty-faced bastard, soaked in Calvados, started on the armchair with a knife. The leader, who was coarse and had a face rather like a bull-dog, grilled my uncle in his broken French, "Where he is, your nephew Delescure? Tell me now. What profession is he? What he doing in your house?"

"He's a commercial traveller and has to travel a lot. He's over twenty-one and I can't answer for his movements."

[1] This motorcycle incident nearly proved disastrous for the unwitting owner. He had left his machine parked by a kerb in Moulins, where it had caught Chantal's eye. She had jumped into the saddle, smiled, and asked her friend to take the photograph. The poor owner was astounded when he was roused at dawn one day at Montluçon by a posse of Gestapo agents, who arrested him, roughed him up, and interrogated him for a gruelling twenty-four hours. He could not understand what they were getting at, but finally managed to clear himself. No sooner was he released than he sold the machine.

"Ach, so. You are not being curious, eh? What about the Tolédano nephews? They in business too?"

"They were here on holiday."

"You make me laugh. Shut up with your rubbish. You are answering bad, so get the coat and come. Your house full of spies and terrorists."

So Uncle Freddy was taken off to Moulins prison which was locally known as "Heartbreak Hotel". The head of the Vichy Gestapo interrogated him for eight hours. He never flinched, never contradicted himself, but remained clear-headed and calm, the whole time looking his interrogator straight in the eyes. He was not manhandled but he was not fed. He was questioned in bad French and Uncle Freddy stuck to his guns in perfect German. Then a very odd thing happened. The Kriminaloffizier from Vichy asked, "I suppose you're a Catholic, like all Frenchmen?"

"No, I'm a Protestant."

"Oh, I see. Well, sit down, won't you?"

The German policeman's attitude changed instantly, which was strange because religion had nothing to do with the interrogation. He offered my uncle a cigarette, called him Monsieur Passy, and dropped his offensive tone. He soon appeared to be convinced as to Uncle Freddy's sincerity. He let him go, saying, "Now be very careful. Our information is reliable and we know for a fact that this Delescure is a dangerous terrorist. He goes about armed and is likely to kill you if you let him near you, so I'm warning you. He knows we're on his tail and may well return to your house. Let him in, but notify us immediately. We'll pick him up and rid you of the menace. We know all about the three of them. Yves is a silly young man, but Claude is a real terrorist."

[V]

The door opened and a ray of light shot suddenly into the cell.
The outline of a man in German uniform appeared against the
light for a moment before the door gently closed. He slowly
approached the pallet where I lay. I tried to roll over on one
side and hoist myself up on my elbow, but I had forgotten that
before I passed out my hands had been firmly secured behind
me. Schultz had first drenched me to the skin with cold water
to bring me round, and then locked my wrists into a pair of
terrible handcuffs whose sharp jaws bit into my flesh like a pair
of fox traps. My effort to move revived all the agonizing pain.
How long had they tortured me? When had the Gestapo arrested
me? When had I fallen into this abyss? Was it only yesterday?
I just couldn't remember. My head had been so bashed about
that I'd lost all sense of time.

The man stood still beside me and laid a hot, podgy hand on
my forehead. "Don't move and don't try to talk," he whispered.
"I am a German medical orderly, Brother Alfred of the Order of
Saint Francis. I have come to look after you and make you a
little more comfortable."

I knew better than to believe him. I had heard and seen too
much in the last two days. It was just another Gestapo trick,
but dirtier than all the others.

"Why don't you get it over with, and kill me quickly? I won't
talk. I've told you all I know. I have nothing to confess. Tell
those two that sent you, Ernst and Schultz, they're wasting their
time. For God's sake, if that still means anything to you, let me
die alone. Just get out . . ."

The very presence of this impostor shattered all my pride and
resistance.

"You don't understand. You must trust me. By the name of
Christ I swear that I really am an orderly and a Franciscan. I
am here to comfort you, with the help of God. I heard about you

from the French head warder. 'Go to Number 67,' he said. 'The Gestapo have beaten the poor wretch to a pulp. He can't sit or stand and you're the only one who can help him.' So here I am."

He fished out a tiny torch from his pocket and flashed it on the cross he wore beneath his tunic next to his skin. Then he showed me his missal and his papers. What really convinced me, however, was his eyes. They were incredibly kind and gentle. His round, pink face bore a calm and peaceful smile that radiated peace. It was a guileless monk's face.

Was this really an answer to last night's prayers? Had he really come to rescue me when all seemed lost, when I was on the brink of death and despair? Had this messenger of Christ that stood beside me in my cell really come to help me?

"Come along, my friend," he said affectionately, "Alfred will take you to the infirmary and look after you. You'll be much more comfortable and we'll be able to talk. I've seen your brother Yves. He is chained up in a cell down below. He blames himself for your arrest. He thinks that you must loathe him for it..."

"Of course I don't! God, how awful! It wasn't like that at all."

I couldn't stand. My legs were so swollen that they filled my trousers to bursting. Shreds of cloth hung from the bits of skin that had stretched and split open beneath the blows struck by Ernst and his henchmen. I tried to drag myself to the door but my strength gave out. The handcuffs prevented me from steadying myself, and before the Franciscan could catch me I keeled over into the open slop pail. It was agony, but I picked myself up. The Franciscan's sad smile expressed the full meaning of the word *compassion* in its true Latin sense: this man was suffering *with* me.

"Wait a minute," he said. "We mustn't be seen. If Alfred were caught, what would become of his other prisoners?"

He looked up and down the corridor and leant over the handrail. The way was clear.

"If we run into a German guard, I'll pretend to be shoving you around. We mustn't look suspicious. What I am doing is strictly forbidden. But we needn't worry about the French guards."

Brother Alfred helped me along, almost carrying me all the way to the infirmary. I could never have made it on my own. He was red in the face and sweating heavily, bursting at the seams of his overtight uniform, as he literally lifted me along the last few yards, gripping me as he did so under the armpits. His hands were grasping the muscles that had torn when Peter Emmerich had strung me up by the wrists, and I bit into my lip to stifle a scream of pain. My strength was ebbing. I tried to speak but couldn't hear myself. I could only just see Alfred through a muggy haze. I thought I was dying . . .

I came to on a chair. Alfred was leaning over me anxiously. "Thank God you're still alive," he said. "You passed out. I'm afraid I haven't as much as a lump of sugar to give you to eat."

He fumbled in his tunic and finally brought out a sort of key or tin-opener with which he tried to open my handcuffs. He was pouring with sweat, and became so flustered that he bent the key. It was my turn to calm him down. "Easy does it. Turn it the right way up. Steady on . . ."

The jaws snapped open, and he gently eased the saw teeth out of my skin. My left hand was bright purple and twice its normal size. A deep welt divided it from the rest of my arm; it started to bleed again and the blood dripped on to Alfred's sleeve. As the circulation returned to my stiff fingers my fingertips prickled as though stung by an army of red ants.

Alfred Stanke—he had just told me his name—tried to peel off my clothes. It was no easy task, as I could do little more than sit and shiver.

He felt quite sick when he saw my back, which was a mass of black, festering welts left by the lash.

"Armer Kerl! Mein lieber Gott, mein lieber Gott! Marc, my poor Marc," he kept saying. "What swine! What filthy swine! Alfred has seen their work before, but nothing like this."

"Surely Yves is worse off?"

"No, not half as bad."

My knees were the size of my thighs, and my shins were black with bruises and dried blood. The skin on my shoulders was in shreds and bleeding; in places it had simply ripped off. One of my eyes was closed and I couldn't see much out of the other. My head looked as though it had been used as a punch-ball. My

[66]

fingers were especially sore. Schultz had not pounded me much, but his ruler had caught me sharply on the nails. I had not been able to react quickly enough each time I saw it lashing down.

Alfred tended my wounds with his round, experienced hands, so accustomed to touching and feeling, to relieving and curing. He spread a sweet-smelling ointment on them that brought instant relief.

"I brought this cream back from our Caritas hospital in Cologne. It is a recipe of the Poor Clare nuns. It soothes away the pain."

He cleaned the larger wounds with ether. His touch was surprisingly gentle and light for a man of his size. He gave me his missal and said, "Here, write your address down on one of the pages so that I can get in touch with your parents."

I could not hold a pen and had to dictate my address to him. Since his French was not up to much, I had to spell it all out in German. Although he had been in France for three years, he knew about ten words of the language. His native German was not much easier to understand. He spoke a gritty Rhine dialect that had many strange inflections. I was only familiar with Southern German and found it all the harder to follow his peculiar mixture of *Plattdeutsch* and *Hochdeutsch*. Moreover, he never said "I'll do this" or "I think so and so", but rather "Alfred will do this" and "Alfred thinks so and so". This was not conceit but his own peculiar way of speaking.

"Who are you? Why are you, a Franciscan, risking your life for strangers and enemies of your country?"

"Any man in trouble is Alfred's friend, regardless of his colour, religion, origins, nationality, regardless of what he's done to get him into prison. The greater his reasons for being here, the more likely he is to be loved and understood by Alfred.

"People in distress, such as you, Marc, are Alfred's life and joy. When he comforts them, they help Alfred to do his duty. It is very difficult to act alone and in secret. Alfred brings comfort and he receives affection in exchange. I know what I have to do. I am only obeying the rules of Saint Francis."

His eyes glowed as he mentioned St Francis. When I looked at this great, round Rabelaisian monk with his large, ruddy face and his jovial smile, I found it hard to imagine him as a lay brother wandering about St Damian monastery on Umbria's holy hill amid the peace of Franciscan Assisi. I couldn't picture him as one of the figures in Giotto's frescoes in the Chiesa Superiore.

As he talked and talked in his sing-song way, I began to understand his complicated turns of phrase. He told me about himself, about his childhood in Danzig, where he had been born some thirty-nine years before, about his chosen vocation and about his parents.

He also told me about his experiences with men of the French Resistance, the 'saboteurs' and 'terrorists' and 'spies' who had been imprisoned in the Bordiot since 1942.

"It has been a very rewarding experience to know these men from all walks of life, Communists, atheists, the lot, and brothers to a man. It has been a joy and a blessing for Alfred."

"Aren't you afraid the Gestapo will find you out?"

"God will see to that. Besides, they are really awfully stupid and Alfred is quite cunning. He's got something up here," he replied, tapping his forehead with his finger. "But if it is God's will that I be found out, then I'll try to face death as bravely as all the Frenchmen I've seen being led away at dawn."

He told me about the men he had known. Some had been shot, some deported. He told me some of the detainees' names, though he usually completely mispronounced them, and kept on asking, "Do you know him? What about Farenc, and Desgeorges, and Arnold?"

I felt these men really were his friends. He had helped them and shared their misfortunes. His 'catalogue' included all sorts of people: politicians such as Senator Plaisant, who was tortured in the rue Michel-de-Bourges, senior ranking officers such as Colonel Haegelen, working men, Jews, rich tradesmen, pimpernels caught smuggling people across the frontier, ecclesiastics such as Canon Le Guen, the dean of the cathedral, and doctors such as Dr Mérigot of Vierzon.

Alfred had a kind word to say about each of them and regretted that he could not do more for some of them. He repeated over and over again, "Alfred thanks the Lord daily for letting him know such men."

He explained his connections with the dignitaries of Bourges,

[68]

with the Prefecture, with the Archbishop's palace, with Monsignor Lefebvre, and with the venerable Abbé Moreux, whose textbooks on astronomy were prescribed reading at school. The poor fellow had just spent a few weeks in the Bordiot.

He told me how he carried messages back from released prisoners to those still inside by a system which he operated with Félix Desgeorges, a wine wholesaler, and Georges Ruetsch, the interpreter at the Prefecture.

"Thanks to Georges Ruetsch, who is remarkably well informed, we can let the prisoners know about every arrest made by the Gestapo and also tell prisoners' families of their whereabouts and fates."

Alfred went to the homes of both of these men, and always managed to smuggle a few supplies back. He had a way in everywhere.

"When I need to be immersed in prayer, I go to my French brothers in their monastery in the rue Porte-Jaune and with them I ask the Lord to help me in my work. I go several times a week, daily if I can."

He told me the most incredible stories.

"Not long ago my friend Georges Ruetsch told me that the Resistance was preparing an attack on Bourges prison to save the latest batch of condemned men. I offered to give him inside information and to assist the operation, but I finally had to advise Ruetsch to call the whole thing off because they didn't have the means to succeed."

I started wondering if Alfred might turn out to be the local Resistance movement's *eminence grise*. Brilliant casting if he were, and if not, the results were the same, perhaps even better still. For three years now, with no weapons but his cross of mercy, he had done for France what few others had dared do.

"You see, Marc," he smiled, "I too have had a spell in prison. I was arrested in 1936 by the Gestapo and imprisoned in Coblenz. One day in March the SS requisitioned the religious orders' lodgings and property, and arrested all the monks in my monastery. I spent ten days in a cell with a pimp and a murderer. I myself was not knocked about much, but I saw what the Gestapo did to others. My hatred of Nazism and of these sadistic Nazi brutes dates from my own first-hand experience. I

[69]

studied their methods and got to know how they operated. I realized then," he continued, "that it is essential to keep up the prisoners' morale right from the moment when they are still dazed by the shock of being arrested. They must at all costs be prevented from giving up everything and plunging into despair. I've seen men withstand the first round of Gestapo interrogation without giving an inch, and then crack during the next few days and delight their torturers by confessing to all sorts of imaginary crimes. This is why I worked out a system of communication with my friend Ruetsch. We keep prisoners in touch with their families and with one another, and we tell them how to defend themselves and who to use as alibis. We have saved quite a few from the firing squad."

Brother Alfred told me about two men from Berry, Péru and Arnold,[1] who were caught and imprisoned when the Germans uncovered a Resistance network. They were put in separate cells, but Alfred arranged for them to meet. In this way they made their stories tally before the Gestapo could set to work on them individually, and Arnold was therefore not tried and condemned at Bourges, as he would otherwise have been.

I was already quite astonished, but when he described how he operated I was afraid for his life. He arranged to be on night duty as often as he could, either by bribing the guards or by innocently offering to stand in for them while they went off for a night of women and drinking in the town. He made them pay him for his services so as not to arouse their suspicions, and then saved the money in order to buy food for the prisoners. As a result, he was usually in sole command of the Bordiot at night, and even went so far as to smuggle in Ruetsch to visit the prisoners in their cells, right under the sentries' noses.

I could not decide which to admire most in this man, his courage or his kindness. Had he ever been caught, our mutual enemy, the Gestapo, would have been merciless. What I had suffered was mere child's play by comparison with the treatment he would have received. There would be a mockery of a trial in which he would be vilified, degraded, insulted, humiliated, called a Communist, a traitor, a saboteur, showered with curses from

[1] Monsieur Arnold came from Alsace, and was horribly tortured by Paoli for refusing to admit that he was German.

[70]

the filthy Nazi vocabulary. He would have died by the axe or the rope at one of those Berlin prisons that specialized in that sort of thing: Moabit, Spandau,[1] or Ploetzensee.

At the Bordiot, where informing was rife, Brother Alfred must have come under constant surveillance. He was an ecclesiastic, a monk who lent a helping hand to Resistance prisoners, the worst possible crime in a world of concentration camps. His movements must have been watched, reported, recorded. He must have had immense faith and been very resourceful to carry out his mission in such adverse conditions.

This German Franciscan loved his country. His patriotism in no way conflicted with his faith. He made it quite clear to me that he was born a German and a German he remained. He refused to accept a Germany disfigured and degraded by the Nazis, the Gestapo, and the SS. He was a simple man who lived his life by the maxim "Love thy neighbour." Simple, yes, but not a simpleton. He knew the gospels well, and his favourite quotation was from the Epistle of St John, which he said always served him as a guiding example: "We ought to lay down our lives for the brethren. . . . If any man say: I love God, and he hateth his brother, he is a liar."

Brother Alfred did not trouble with dogma, or canon law, or theology. He knew I was a Protestant, because I told him, but he never asked me what my beliefs were nor tried to influence them. Religious differences were no problem: I was in distress, and so became his brother in Christ.

I began to feel that I had known this portly, jovial, communicative monk all my life. There was something of the peasant about him: his eyes that wrinkled at the corners as if he were used to scanning the horizon, his salty turns of phrase, his solid common sense. I could see him in the blue overalls that farmers in the Berry wear, with a big, black beret on his head and soil under his fingernails. He was obviously fond of food and drink. "A drop of Sancerre wine would perk you up," he would say.

As I listened to him speaking in that frank, ingenuous way, I felt a wave of peace wash over me. The pain began to ebb away, the nightmare began to fade. Life reasserted itself.

[1] Paul Ruetsch, Georges Ruetsch's brother, was shot by the Nazis at Spandau on February 13th, 1945.

I started considering the ways in which men are singled out and entrusted with missions. I was absolutely positive, after that revelation in my cell just a short while before, that Alfred was a chosen man. Had there been no war, he would have carried on in his humdrum provincial monastery near Heidelberg. His very retiring nature, his upbringing, his surroundings, would never have singled him out for greater things. But God transforms his chosen men: witness some of the prophets. Saul of Tarsus, for example, was a Pharisee and scourge of Christians and was transformed into St Paul. He became the first missionary. Such matters are beyond my ken, but I was certain that Alfred was such an example of God's divine intervention.

"What about Yves?" I asked anxiously. "What have they done to him? How is he?"

"I wasn't able to see him before tonight and then only for a minute from the doorway while the guard was changing. I had to be very careful. He is in solitary confinement in a cell in the basement. He is thought to be a dangerous terrorist and is under close guard at night as well as during the day. He's very depressed, but not as badly hurt as you. That's all I can tell you about him."[1]

I then told Alfred of the insane way Claude and I had carried on in Bourges, and then of my equally mad visit to the Gestapo.

"We must pray that your cousin is safe," said Alfred. "These brutes will go to any lengths to find him. You were out of your mind to walk right into their lair, you know."

"All I could think of was rescuing Yves."

"My dear friend, nothing can save a man once they've got him in their clutches. But rest assured that Alfred will do everything he possibly can for your brother."

The prison clock struck five. The September night was beginning to pale and it was time to return to my cell. I had been with my heaven-sent friend for three hours. Brother Alfred had done

[1] Alfred later confessed to me, "I shall never forget what your brother looked like that night. I could just see his face in the darkness through the bars. He looked so terribly helpless and desperate, and he kept mumbling, 'Thank you, thank you, dear Father, thank you.' I couldn't help crying. It was like an apparition and it kept me awake for days. I shall never forget it as long as I live."

his best to patch me up with his scant medical aids, and my worst wounds had been cleaned and disinfected with ether.

"I do have some mercurochrome but I don't think I should use it. If the Gestapo saw your face covered with red smears they would put two and two together and I would end up in a cell too."

I shook with anger again. "The filthy swine, they're even more bestial than I thought."

My left wrist, gouged by the sharp fangs of the handcuffs, was a bleeding, pulpy mess. The Franciscan feared that the bone had been damaged. My breastbone felt as though it had been crushed and breathing was something like eating fire.

Alfred had to put my handcuffs back on before we left the Infirmary. He eased them on gently, leaving the chains as slack as he could.

Then he undertook the Herculean task of hauling me back to the cell. He hoisted me on to his back and stumbled along, puffing and blowing under the load. We stopped every three yards or so. We must have made an odd pair—the stout soldier-monk dragging along the tattered remains of a man, in the diffused light of black-out bulbs that set the stairwell girders gleaming cold blue. I groaned with each step he took. On the first floor, devoted to civil crimes, we encountered a French warder. Alfred and he exchanged a brief, knowing nod and we went on. Alfred heaved me up one last time and got me into my cell, where he eased me on to my pallet.

I felt desperate. "Don't go, Brother Alfred. Stay a little while longer."

"Alfred must go now. It's late and he has to try to see your brother. Alfred is a night-owl and his work is not yet finished. He will then catch the Paris train to fix up a meeting with your parents. He'll be back with you tomorrow night. God bless you. God is all-seeing and all-knowing. He will help you."

The Franciscan seemed as upset as I was. He held me close to him before tucking me maternally under the rough blanket that reeked of institutional mothballs. Then he slipped away as noiselessly as he had entered.

[VI]

It was impossible to get to sleep. My mind was working over-time, I had so much to sort out. The sudden appearance of the monk in the horrific series of events which had overtaken me during the last few days confused me. I tried to think clearly and discern some logic behind it all, but it was an immense effort as I was feeling feverish. Gradually reason started seeping through. I was amazed when I began to realize that my suffer-ings had given way to a growing feeling of inner peace rather than to the expected angry revolt. My surprise encounter with the Franciscan had revived my childhood faith, which had undergone an eclipse during my earlier imprisonment. It gave me new hope. Alfred had made me a richer man and his faith was something I knew would survive my present misfortunes, if I did.

I felt as though St Paul might be asking me what he asked of the Galatian Christians when they were deserting Christ, "Did you experience so many sufferings in vain?"

I knew that I would be eternally indebted to Alfred, and gave thanks to God.

When one's safety-rope snaps within inches of the summit, one's fall is all the more terrible. I suddenly lapsed into a dread-ful fever. My bruised body burnt, my nerves snapped, and I fell into a state of delirium. An enormous pressure tightened round my head. My ears pounded. My mind wandered. I had the sensation of being sucked down a narrowing funnel. Millions of sparks burst through my brain to be extinguished by a volley of black dots that wriggled before my eyes like tadpoles in a spring pond. This was the after-effect of Schultz's 'Son et Lumière'.

The four walls of my cell closed about me, I was isolated within a solitary, petrified fever that made my guts shrivel and contract. I was really frightened. That first day in prison was the longest day of my life, and I was convinced it was my last. I thought these were my death throes.

The fear and pain were driving me mad. My body was frozen stiff, my muscles paralysed. Delirium really does banish reason. It consumes one totally. My skull echoed with ghastly sounds, with snatches of music, snatches of Bach's Toccata in D minor that had the ominous ring of death. I tossed and turned in a demented effort to escape this infernal stranglehold. All I succeeded in doing was further lacerating my wrists with the vicious handcuffs. Then I had a vision of Ernst's monstrous face, grimacing and shouting, "Confess. Where were you on the first?" I screamed for help. I cried. I shivered and sweated. I soaked in my own cold sweat that soon permeated the wood-shaving mattress, already flattened and worn thin by dozens of poor prisoners before me. It occurred to me that I probably had blood-poisoning. I could feel the germs devouring me. My blood was rotting and spreading through my whole system. I was dying. Schultz and Ernst wouldn't have to finish me off—gangrene would soon set in and that would be that.

I knew that this was quite possible, as I had had blood-poisoning and gas-gangrene in 1936 after a minor accident and my foot was only saved by a massive dose of propidon. There was no hope of getting any propidon here.

But no—I would die, certainly, but I would die of thirst. Every inch of me demanded water. I had been thirsty like this in 1941, when I had escaped in Germany, but I was fit and well then and I had managed to hold it in check and survive.

My throat was too parched to cry out. I had fantasies of leaping fountains, dripping rain forests, and rushing waterfalls. My tongue was hard and stony in my mouth, my swollen lips were cracked and dry, and all I could taste was dried blood. For a glass of water, for a mere spoonful, I would have confessed to anything. Then, as though to torment me further, I saw a wretched brass tap sprouting defiantly from the wall. It shone brightly against the whitewash where previous prisoners had scribbled the usual puerile phrases, and where desperate condemned men had left their last messages: "Death to my murderers," "This is my last night. Farewell," "Goodbye, Jacqueline. We'll meet again in Heaven," "I am going to my death, betrayed by a neighbour," and so on.

I tried to drag myself to the tap, which was only a couple of yards away. But two yards proved too far. Had I gone on trying I would have collapsed on the tiled floor and never risen again. I called out for Alfred, for my mother, my father. Sheer panic made my whole body tremble.

Then, about twelve hours later, when I had given up all hope, when I had stopped fighting the pain and had come to accept the prospect of an animal's death, a German corporal came in on his rounds.

"A glass of water, for pity's sake," I pleaded.

I think he was shocked by what he saw. He undid my handcuffs for ten minutes and gave me a drink. He may have taken pity on me or he may have thought I would die and he would have to answer for my death.

"You poor fellow. Tomorrow you are to be given food and water, but you're in solitary today."

"Tomorrow may be too late. One still gets thirsty in solitary confinement, you know."

"I'm sorry, but I have my orders. If it was up to me . . ."

"How is my brother?"

"He's all right. His morale is good."

I could have hugged that German NCO. When I was alone again I felt there might be some hope left. I still had a raging temperature, but my head had cleared, a false lucidity which often comes with high temperatures. I realized that only a miracle could save me and that Yves was beyond hope: he would be shot. If I managed to recover from the after-effects of the torture, and if I did not die from gangrene, I would be wakened one day at the crack of dawn by the sound of jack-boots, and they would carry me off to the firing range. I would face the firing squad as that flap-eared Neanderthal thug had told me I would. I would not have a trial or be sent to Germany. The Gestapo was obviously convinced that I was a master-mind and Yves a pawn. Alfred had warned me that I was listed as a dangerous terrorist. Alfred had also gathered that Yves had been put in the punishment cell to pay for his lies. I was a prize catch; Claude, however, remained their public enemy number one.

Alfred described the punishment cell and I trembled for Yves. It was where they put the trouble-makers. It was a small, damp

[76]

dungeon with an iron grill on the door, as in the days of the
Man in the Iron Mask. The prisoner was manacled with balls
and chains behind these bars. A shuttered peep-hole was the only
contact with life and this was opened from the outside by a
warder. He had a plank bed with no mattress or blankets. Food
was passed through the bars: a bowl of water a day and a hunk
of mouldy bread every three. There were hordes of fleas and, of
course, rats. Only a savage could have conceived of such loathsome quarters. How and why on earth did we ever get ourselves
involved with such filth?

It was futile to regret our fates. I thought of my parents. My
mother had been terrified for her sons ever since 1939. My
brother Guy was still a prisoner in Germany, and though Yves
and I had got out of that we had only ended up in a worse mess.
My parents would feel terrible when Alfred told them of our
plight. I hoped and prayed they would not take him for a
Gestapo agent.

I relived my childhood and quiet, happy, youthful days, and
recalled it all with that heightened sharpness that fever brings.
I saw our Christmas-trees at Saint-Germain-en-Laye, and the
puddings that my mother made in the traditional English way. I
relived my Boy Scout days. I remembered all my friends from
high-school, from the School of Political Sciences, from Law
School, from Saumur.[1] A kaleidoscope of twenty happy, pre-
War years turned before me. All that had come to an end the
previous evening in the rue Michel-de-Bourges.

Suddenly, and as silently as at his first visit, Alfred appeared
beside me. He moved about in the dark with the gentle stealth of
a cat, but his presence seemed to light up my cell. He took my
pulse, and I detected an anxious note in his voice.

"My dear boy, you have a temperature of a hundred and
four. We must do something at once. I'll go for help."

Five minutes later he returned with the NCO who had given
me the water. He put on the light. Alfred, who was only a

---

[1] Some of the faces were blurred, others as sharp and clear as if they
were standing there before me, like that of Jean-Claude Schreiber, a brilliant student at the School of Political Sciences, who always came top in
the Army exams and knew more than his NCO instructor.

medical orderly, gave his superior sharp orders: "First take off
his handcuffs. Give him the medicine and something to drink.
He must be kept warm or he will get pneumonia, or worse."

The other man, who answered to the name of Paul, did not
protest and did as he was told. The two of them tried to make
me more comfortable. They brought me warm herbal tea and
aspirin. They rubbed my chest with a counter-irritant and
tended to my damaged wrist.

Paul agreed to let me have my arms in front of me. This was
a great relief as I could not have borne having them behind my
back much longer. Then the NCO left me alone with the Franciscan and wished me well.

"What a fright. You looked ghastly. You were turning green,
but your colour is coming back a little now. Poor boy, how old
are you?"

"Twenty-six."

"You look eighteen. You're all skin and bone. When did you
last eat?"

"I can't remember. About three days ago."

"We'll soon remedy that. I've got a few things for you and
your mother has given me more." His pockets bulged with
treasures which he emptied on to my pallet: fruit, biscuits,
chocolate, cheese, and ham.

"I have as much again for your brother in my other pockets.
Your mother also wanted you both to have one of these."

It was a New Testament. She had marked parts of the Gospel
of St Matthew: "Blessed are ye, when men shall revile you, and
persecute you . . . Blessed are the merciful . . ."

I felt a lump in my throat. Then he took a letter from my
mother out of his wallet and handed it to me. I took it, trembling.
Only she could write such affectionate, understanding letters. She
must have written it with a sinking heart but there was no sign
of her own sadness. She did not complain. She did not judge.
She wrote as she always did when her loved ones were away
from her, doing her best to put us back in the family picture.
She made me feel she knew I should soon be home again. She
gave me news about my friends, about our cat Minoche who had
just had kittens. She told me how she had just been making jam,
how my uncle had had to get the harvest in himself that year

and that his tractor had broken down, how my father had a bad cold . . .

I had received hundreds of letters like this one during the three years I had been a prisoner of war. I used to keep them in my pocket for days, reading and re-reading them whenever I had a few minutes to myself: in the fields of Jagstheim and Neiderstetten alone with my horse and plough, in the German forests while I was escaping, in the punishment cell at Hammelburg.

The writing began to swim before my eyes, and Alfred, sensing my emotion, kept absolutely quiet. At last he said, "You are a lucky man, Marc, to have such a mother. So wunderbar, so wunderbar," he kept saying. "And they both speak such marvellous German, your mother especially. It made things much easier for me."

He had been deeply impressed by his meeting with my parents. They had arranged to meet in the café at the Gare du Nord. My father's twin brother had gone along with them. My mother had recoiled at the sight of his uniform, but Alfred understood and accepted her initial reaction.

"I know how the French feel about us. So many dreadful things have been done by men wearing this uniform that it is not surprising that you should lump us all together. I am used to it now. When I go to see prisoners' families I am sometimes flung out on my ear. It's a risk I must take and I accept the consequences. On the other hand, I will tell you a story that partially redeems some of our men. It happened here at the Bordiot in 1942, before I arrived. There was a German guard of Polish extraction called Novack and a certain Girouille of the Berry Resistance who was condemned to death. Novack was in the firing squad. He refused to fire because it was against his principles, so he was placed alongside Girouille and shot with him. They were both buried in the Saint-Lazare cemetery. He was a very brave man and died to save his conscience.

"I have visited many families since I came here, and I have always been the bearer of bad news. But I have never yet come across such kind, brave people as your parents. They are such interesting, cultivated people. It was a rewarding experience for a humble Franciscan like me."

I thought I detected a certain note of pride in his voice as he said this. He told me that my father was going to move heaven and earth to get me out. He was going to bring my case to the attention of Marshal Pétain, to Abetz's German office in Paris, to the Swiss Embassy, and goodness knows where else. I thought my father was living on illusions as far as Yves and I were concerned.[1]

"Oh, I nearly forgot. I bought you a toothbrush and some soap. I'll get you some more things later. You can't go short of everything like this."

Then he told me what he had been up to. "Meeting your parents really upset me. I felt that you two boys were in an awful mess, that your cases were exceptionally tragic. I was so touched by your mother and father and I respected them so much that I was determined to do something to save you. I knew that both of you would be interrogated again. It's the usual thing and I know them. They're never satisfied with half the story, they want all the details. The first thing to do is make your stories sound convincing and above all tally. Yves will have to stop spinning tales that only implicate everyone, especially you. Suddenly I thought of a solution. I have a very dear friend, Abbé Jean Barut,[2] who was arrested at Bourges and whom I helped out of the Bordiot. He was just the man for the job. When I left your parents I went to see him in his parish in north Paris, at Persan-Beaumont."

He proceeded to describe the outcome of his venture: "The Abbé was in the middle of a catechism class when his anxious housekeeper rushed in, saying, 'Father, there's a German officer to see you downstairs. I told him you were out but he wouldn't believe me. He won't go away. He is standing down there nodding and smiling all the while. He's probably come to take you off again. You must hurry and get away.' "

[1] The very next day my father took the train to Bourges and called on the Gestapo. It was becoming a family trait! They questioned him at length and finally Schultz let him go after commiserating with him for having sired such awful sons: Yves a liar and a spy and me a stuck-up, dangerous terrorist. Father was not deterred by this set-back, but went on to Vichy, where he got as far as seeing an officer in the Military Government who gave him vague assurances that something would be done about us. His efforts were no more rewarded than this.

[2] See Appendices, p. 167.

OF BOURGES

The Abbé was somewhat puzzled by his housekeeper's odd account. He tiptoed down the stairs and spied his old friend the Franciscan through the half-open door. They embraced fondly like long-lost brothers.

"My goodness, you did give me a fright," scolded Abbé Barut. "What on earth are you doing here?"

"Jean, my dear friend, I've come on a rather serious errand. I remember you saying once that you would always be ready to do me a favour. Well, now I've come to ask your help. It's a question of a man's life—two men's lives, actually. They are brothers and in prison in Bourges for spying. The younger one is in the punishment cell, and you know what that means—he's confessed to all sorts of incriminating nonsense under torture and has implicated his brother. I want you, my brother in Christ, to come with me to Bourges to meet the boy in the Bordiot, build up his morale, and explain to him in French exactly what he has to say to the Gestapo. He must learn his story by heart."

"My dear man, you can't be serious. Even if, by some miracle, I did get into the prison, how would I ever get out again?"

"Leave that to me. I've worked it all out. I have a set of duplicate keys and friends inside. You won't be the first friend I've smuggled in and out to do this sort of thing. Ask our friend Ruetsch if you don't believe me."

"Well, in that case, of course I'll come. But I would only do this for you, you know, Alfred."

Abbé Barut did not even stop to remove his cassock. They took the next train to Bourges. Alfred paid their fares, but they travelled in separate first-class compartments, and walked through the barriers separately, arriving in Bourges before the curfew.

"Follow me, but on the other side of the street," Alfred told him. They met again in Alfred's room, where they spent a few minutes in meditation and prayer before going into action.

At the time fixed by Alfred, half-past midnight, they set out for the prison, keeping as before to different sides of the street. At one point they saw a German patrol ahead of them. Alfred marched towards it to allay possible disaster, waving his arms, barking out orders, and even pulling out his gun to fire a shot in the air. The patrol vanished into the night. Alfred opened the

[81]

main door of the prison with the official key. He exchanged a
few words with the French head warder Douzou, who seemed to
take the Franciscan's unorthodox comings and goings in his
stride. Abbé Barut remembered his stint there nine months pre-
viously and shrank visibly.

"There's no need to worry. I'm standing in for one of the
warders on duty tonight."

Nevertheless, the Franciscan took the extra precaution of
locking his friend into the sickroom cupboard.

"I shan't be long. Say an 'Our Father' or an 'I confess' in
the meantime." He smiled.

Yves was asleep on the floor of the punishment cell and could
not understand what Alfred was up to.

"When I took him up to Barut," said Alfred, "your brother
cried with emotion. He kept embracing the Abbé and me and
thanking us, laughing and crying at the same time. Even Abbé
Barut, who is a tough character who's been through a lot himself, nearly broke down and cried. Everything went smoothly.
Yves now knows what he must say when they question him
again. I also got him a shower at two o'clock which did him the
world of good. I took the Abbé back to my place to rest before
going back to Paris in the morning. And now it's half-past three
and I've had a tiring day. You must get some sleep too. You are
not alone, Marc, you see. We are all thinking of you and Yves
and things are being done. It is God's will."

When Alfred stood up to leave, I asked him the question that
had haunted me when I was delirious: "What do you think will
become of us, Alfred?"

"You will probably be sent for trial and might get away with
ten years, but Yves's position is very tricky. The Gestapo don't
like spies and gun-runners. He really worries me."

"Do you mean he may be sentenced to death?" I hardly
dared say the words because I was afraid to hear his answer.

"I'm afraid he may be. Put your trust in God and pray for
Yves as I pray for both of you. His life is in God's hands."

How incredibly lucky Yves and I were to have such a friend
at such a time. Alone, we would have been lost.

The Gestapo had learnt from experience that a prisoner left
on his own in total solitude soon succumbs to despair, regret,

[82]

doubt, and depression. He is then ready to sign all manner of confessions. If that failed they would resort to such a time-honoured trick as the planting of a stool-pigeon, who would insinuate himself into the prisoner's confidence, promptly double-cross him, and deliver him whole to the wolves.

I woke feeling as though I had been through a mincing machine. I was black and blue and all my joints felt dislocated. My ears still rang and my eyes could not focus properly. I was too weak to move my head. I had slept only fitfully after the Franciscan had left me, but my temperature was down thanks to his timely intervention.

The first visitor of the day was the slopman. He was the oldest political detainee in the Bordiot, a chatty Czech called Vladimir Letosky, known to us all as Joseph. He spoke the weirdest French, highly spiced with slang and swearwords. "Bloody Huns," he swore, "what the slobs done to you? No possible hit someone like that. Not done. They tell me new prisoner been worked over real good, but shit, man, this is too much. Here, they no hurt you, them good fellers, 'cept for Kurt Michel from Alsace. Him real nasty, stinking bastard. But old Alfred makes up for him, real friend, real nice man, and always around when someone hurt. Real respected round here, believe me, he really is. And your brother, he says hello. Is it real you two being bloody terrorists?"

He slammed the door before I could answer, then he poked his head round again and said cheerily, "Tomorrow, me slip you some bread."

"For heaven's sake, come on," bawled the lance-corporal with him. This was Gustav, a down-to-earth country bumpkin with a large, red face and a drunkard's nose. He was quite out of place in the prison, and was much more interested in wine and women than in the pleasures of being a warder.

I managed to spill a good three-quarters of the tasteless beverage Joseph had brought me. My handcuffs and my general weakness made me shaky and clumsy.

An hour, perhaps two, went by as I dozed fitfully, shaken awake every so often by fits of shivering.

Alfred had told me that a single cough at my door meant he

[83]

was alone and that three coughs would indicate that he was in bad company, that the Gestapo was with him. Everyone knew Alfred's chain-smoker's cough. He smoked his way through a couple of packets of Gauloises a day, as well as through a good few German cigarettes made of Macedonian straw, and a few cigars. His cough was as famous as that laughter of his which rose from the depths of his stomach and bespoke the lover of good food and wine.

I started to the sound of the triple cough. The key ground in the lock. Ernst Basedow's bloodshot face loomed up in the doorway, while behind him stood the glum-faced Franciscan. My scalp tingled with dread.

"Get up and get out! Interrogation!" bellowed Ernst.

I tried to get up, but just could not make it. Alfred whispered something to Ernst, who said, "All right, all right. Get another warder, then."

Boozy old Gustav and Alfred whisked me up and deposited me at the main entrance. Yves was already there, unshaven and looking as white as a sheet, but his eyes were brighter than they had been and he looked more determined.

Ernst pushed me into the small Citroën II which had a new driver. The same dog, however, lay at my feet. I could not say anything to Yves. We were soon in the courtyard of the Gestapo HQ in the rue Michel-de-Bourges. It looked smaller than I remembered it. We were not taken down to the cellar nor led into the torture room. Instead, Ernst chose to chain us back to back and made us stand in the middle of the courtyard, watched by an SS guard with a drawn pistol.

We must have stood there for about ten minutes, though it seemed longer. We leant against each other and I looked round the place. I became absorbed in the behaviour of the Alsatian dog, which kept sniffing and scratching under the door of some sort of guard room on the right of the entrance, trying to get in.[1] Our SS guard left us for a moment while he chained up the dog. When his back was turned, Yves whispered, "I've seen the priest. I shan't say anything."

We soon discovered the reason for our detention in the court-

---

[1] The Gestapo used this room as a morgue for the bodies of executed men. They were then taken for burial to the Saint-Lazare cemetery.

yard. The rooms were all being used. They had not finished doing their worst to some other poor soul. The victim soon emerged from the cellars. His young face was swollen, and his eyebrows were caked with blood. Before the guards could stop him he whispered to us as he passed, "My name's Boiché.[1] I'm in Cell 100."

They kicked him viciously and threw him into a waiting car as we were taken up to the first floor. My guard dragged me up the stairs by the handcuffs, tugging at them so hard as he climbed that I tripped on every step. They put me in one room and Yves in the next. Schultz was there, as vile as ever, his face twitching ceaselessly. He came over and locked my handcuffs to a ring on the massive table, and pushed me down into a chair. Then he went out and left me to a black-and-tan police dog which may have been the same one that attended my earlier interrogation. I seemed to recognize the yellow eyes. He lay with his muzzle between his paws and watched my every move. Had I budged an inch, I would have been torn to pieces. He was just doing his job, I suppose. The walls were bare save for three photographs of the Gestapo heroes: Hitler, Himmler, and Heydrich, the scourge of Czechoslovakia. A fine, bloodthirsty trio, whose cold gazes seemed to narrow and focus on me.

The dog pricked up his ears. Shouts came from next door, and then I heard them hitting Yves. They laid into him for an hour or perhaps even more, I don't know. At one point a tall, very fair-haired man came in from next door, holding a lash in his hand. "Your brother's a lot tougher than he was the other day," he said. "He's refusing to talk but we'll break him yet."

I later described him to Alfred, who identified him as Max Winterling, the Breslau engineer now in charge of Section 4A responsible for counteracting Communist activities. He was one of the most feared Gestapo chiefs and Paoli's immediate superior, and had played a part in most of the operations against the Resistance in the Cher.

That sadistic bastard Schultz must have wracked his brains for ways of making my waiting period there unbearable. He had tightened the handcuff's round my wounded wrist so that it started to bleed again. Locking me up as he had against the

---

[1] See Appendices, p. 169.

table with but an inch to spare had caused my calves to knot in cramp, my buttocks to strain between sitting and squatting, my back to hunch forward, and my head to duck between my outstretched arms so as to keep my hands on a level with the table. There was nothing I could do. I did try to turn my knees to one side, but the dog stood up, bared his fangs, and began to growl. I just had to maintain the position Schultz had prescribed. I was at the mercy of a dog, and tears of rage and frustration ran down my face.

Meanwhile, they continued hitting Yves, though I did not hear his voice once amid the chorus of mounting hysteria emitted by his disappointed tormentors.

When they brought him into the room where I was sitting he wore a triumphant smile with a trace of mockery at the thugs on either side of him. He was obviously pleased that his silence had restored his standing in my eyes after his earlier "betrayal", as he called it.

And that was all that happened. I was not questioned. Schultz just ignored me, and handed me over to Ernst, who then sat between Yves and myself in the Citroën. We drove through Bourges for a few minutes and then I saw Yves's manacled hands inching toward the door handle.

He must have been out of his mind. He could not possibly contemplate a get-away from the car. It was suicide. Even if he managed to tumble out of the moving car he would have been a dead man before he had moved a yard. I had to stop him, and tried to catch his eye over Ernst's head. Ernst was unaware of Yves's lunacy. Yves did not see me at first because he was concentrating on reaching the handle, but I finally caught his eye. I tried to look as imploring and disapproving as I could. He got the message and his hands fell back on to his lap.

It was a relief to get to the prison. Ernst handed us over to the warders. Yves stumbled towards his dungeon and Paul took me off to Cell 67. I was sure that Alfred would soon be joining Yves and that he would be as proud as I was of his conduct. We had Abbé Barut to thank.

That evening I made the acquaintance of Big Michel, Kurt Michel, the Alsatian. He blasted into my cell yelling "Trousuntshoose". I could not think what he meant, with the result that he pushed me around as though I were some sort of uncomprehending half-wit. What he was shouting with such conviction turned out to be "Trousers and shoes", since there was a prison regulation which stipulated that we had to hand over these articles of clothing at night. They were put out of our reach in the corridors outside, and this was supposed to prevent any attempts at escape.

On my fifth day there Alfred removed my handcuffs, to our mutual joy and relief.

"The captain says you are now listed as an ordinary prisoner."

I lived for my guardian's regular visits, which were usually at night. Thanks to his care and skill my wounds were healing nicely and my torn muscles were mending. I could sit and move my legs about, but when I tried to stand I became giddy. Alfred stuffed me with fruit and vitamins which I knew he paid for out of his own pocket. The warders came by regularly to stare incredulously at my rainbow-hued face, shocked and disgusted by their countrymen's behaviour. They were very kind to me, and never stopped telling me what a brave brother I had. I became aware of the enormous difference between the ordinary German soldier and the Gestapo, the same difference that I had noticed between the German people as a whole and the Nazis during my earlier prisoner-of-war years.

I came across a pin in my cell, which was a great find, as I used it to keep track of the passing days by marking them up on the wall.

Also on the fifth day I heard someone knocking on the other side of my wall, but unfortunately I had forgotten all the Morse code I had learnt as a Boy Scout and could not understand or return my neighbour's communications. I replied with a completely incomprehensible series of bangs with my shoe, at which the fellow got excited and banged out his message again. Alfred told me a little later that it was Jean Delmotte, who had been sentenced to death after Ernst had almost tortured the life out of him. He was an NCO in the Vichy army and had been caught in the possession of a radio transmitter. His days were numbered.

The following morning just before dawn I was startled out of my sleep by a considerable commotion in the corridor outside. Chains clanked, orders rang out, and doors slammed. I soon understood: they were making ready for an execution.

The grim procession stopped at my door. I heard the key turn in the lock and my heart skipped a beat. Death stared me in the face. I froze and felt sick. A booted, helmeted NCO carrying a machine-gun shone a torch into my cell.

"Come on, Delmotte, it's time," he shouted.

"No, not here, you fool," someone called out, rushing up at that moment, "next door."

"Sorry, my mistake."

As I collapsed limply on to my mattress I caught a glimpse of two manacled, broken wretches who were being pushed to their deaths by the soldiers. The inevitable dogs were also present. The ominous sounds proceeded into the next cell, and then the prison fell silent again. I went to pieces. I broke down and had a good cry, giving full rein to all my pent-up feelings. Alfred came in later that morning, red-eyed and looking terribly depressed.

"Isn't it dreadful! I am ill for ages after an execution. Last night they shot three men, including your neighbour Delmotte."

"Yes, I know. They even came into my cell, perhaps on purpose, to scare me. I wouldn't put it past them."

"No, I don't think so. It wasn't the Gestapo, it was the ordinary army guard."

"Don't you ever go along with them?"

"I haven't the heart or the stomach. I can't bear it. It's not part of my job and I wouldn't be allowed to go. I'm not a prison chaplain, I'm only here as an army corporal, a medical orderly and prison warder. I just happen to be a Franciscan. I'm better off like that. I am freer and I don't come under the same scrutiny as a chaplain. It's a French priest who accompanies them to the range. They mow them down with a machine-gun."

We remained silent for a long time. The execution of the three men had shaken us and I had not yet recovered from my own recent brush with death.

"Does Yves know about them?"

"Yes. News travels fast around here. But he's very strong. He still feels confident."

[88]

Alfred did not stay long as he was off to visit the families of the executed men. I admired the man's courage, going out to face the bitter reactions his news would engender in distracted, stunned relatives. If the Gestapo ever got wind of these activities of his they would soon bring them and him to a nasty end.

On the seventh day they brought me a cell-mate, a smooth-cheeked boy with one leg.

"What did they get you for?" was my first question.

"Gunpowder."

"How do you mean, gunpowder?"

"Well, I work in the Pyrotechnic, you see, the Bourges powder works, and I pinched some gunpowder."

"What for?"

"Well, it wasn't for the Resistance, I'll tell you that. I wanted to get rid of some moles in my kitchen garden. The foreman caught me stuffing some into my pocket and turned me in."

"Did they interrogate you?"

"Yes, a month ago. I was taken to the Gestapo's place in the rue Michel-de-Bourges and they knocked me about a bit. They got it into their thick heads that I'd taken the stuff to slip to the Resistance chaps. I don't care a shit about the Resistance, but would they believe me? Well, I hope they'll lay off now and let me go soon. The English are about to land and that'll fix 'em. I've been here for five blasted weeks. I was in Cell 80 with three other blokes. We only had two mattresses between the lot of us."

"What happened to your leg?"

"I lost it in a motorbike accident in 1939."

I liked this youngster. He was cheerful, down to earth, even-tempered, and amusing. He knew a lot about the prison and gave me a good few tips on how to survive there. At least I now had someone to talk to.

"Your brother's got some guts, you know," said Lucien Tessier, my new companion. "Our cell was above the dungeon and we could hear him singing away all day long. I don't know how he keeps it up. There's no light down there, and he only gets a measly old piece of bread every three days. How can they treat a man like that? We don't get much better grub ourselves, though, do we?"

Lucien had a point. The vile muck they brought us at midday was an apology for soup. Our evening tea and bread was hardly edible. These were starvation rations and it was small wonder that I was not recovering very quickly. My eyes felt better but Lucien was a bit shocked when he first saw me.

"They really went to town on you, you poor bastard. Bloody sods. It must've been bloody awful. When they were doing me over I saw them really fixing another poor bastard: they'd wired his tongue to the mains. It was that bloody sod Paoli that done it."

"I know, I've met him. One of these days someone will shoot the mad dog."

Alfred came to see to my back and appeared to be quite satisfied. He did not seem to have much time for my companion, who was wont to burst into colourful rounds of popular anticlericalism. Alfred had little sympathy for such glib chattering and considered him no great patriot. Lucien was not in very serious trouble and thus did not warrant the Franciscan's attention. Alfred reserved his energies, care, and compassion for those who really needed him.

Conversation with Lucien invariably tended to be about the same sort of thing, and I heard endless detailed stories of this jolly rake's progress through the female population of Berry. My skirt-chaser became somewhat tedious at times, but he was pleasant enough and seemed to admire me somewhat, which more or less forced me to take a keen interest in all his escapades. My thoughts, however, were elsewhere.

Every evening old "Trousuntshoose" would roar in for our things. It occurred to me one evening that it was rather silly to rob Lucien nightly of his one shoe, so we did not leave it out. "Trousuntshoose" almost had a fit and demanded the solitary shoe.

The following evening Lucien said, "We'll get our own back on the stupid fat-head." He unstrapped the complicated artificial limb from his knee stump and parked the clumsy contraption by the door. But "Trousuntshoose" did not have a sense of humour.

"What the hell's this thing?" he yelled, with a deepening of his habitually red face.

"You've got both my mate's shoes there tonight. We felt badly about last night so we thought we'd better try to obey orders more strictly."

"Take the bloody thing back inside, you goddam fool. God, you're even more stupid than I thought."

The story soon got round the prison, and Alfred told me that Gustav, Paul, and Franz, as well as the other warders, thought it a great joke. None of them liked Michel.

"Trousuntshoose" was back with us the following afternoon.

"Eggzersize," he barked.

We spent half an hour pacing round and round a tiny, star-shaped courtyard guarded by a sentry-walk above.

[VII]

September 22nd, 1943

We had a new arrival in our cell. He was well dressed, rather too well, in fact. He wore loud, new yellow shoes with thick crêpe soles, and a suit of good cloth. His hair was smarmed down with brilliantine and he reeked of lavender water. He had the appearance of a successful pimp. I could not place him, but I had a feeling I had come across him before, though I could not think where.

"Too slick to be straight, that one. Wonder what he's up to here," whispered my one-legged friend.

"May I introduce myself," said the newcomer, with a strong low-Parisian accent which he had obviously spent his life correcting in vain. "I'm Jean N. They nicked me for black-marketeering. I was slipping the Boche gold and now they claim I was short-changing them. Not that they're far wrong, mind. I passed them a whole load of junk for months and the suckers coughed up nicely. Then they went and got a new bloke who wasn't so stupid. He soon got wise to my deals and put me inside. Just as well, really. It won't do me any harm to lie low till it all blows over."

I did not relish the prospect of living in such close proximity to this slick character. At least Lucien had not tried to persuade me he worked for the Resistance. Jean N. proceeded to unpack his things on to his pallet. The Gestapo had obviously been unusually considerate to him when they picked him up, for he had had time to pack a pair of neatly ironed pyjamas, a change of linen, slippers, food, and tobacco. Lucien gave me a knowing wink. We both refused the cigars he offered us.

I felt uneasy. Nothing added up. "Bet your life he's a stool-pigeon. Just the type," muttered Lucien under his breath.

Jean N. never stopped talking. He got on our nerves, going

[92]

on and on about his latest mistress, a certain Denise, daughter of a Bourges coal-merchant.

"Stuff it, will you?" Lucien finally exploded. "We don't get enough to eat round here to think about women."

Jean N. was taken aback.

"Do you mean to say you two are trying to survive on what they give you? You must be mad or something. I'll get you some grub. How about some of this for a start?" He fished out a bag of fruit and neither of us had the stomach to refuse. "You're not from these parts, are you?" he asked me bluntly.

"No, I'm from Saint-Germain-en-Laye."

"No, really? Isn't that something, now? I lived there for eight years. I went to school there, left in the fifth form."

"When were you there?"

"1926 to 1930."

"Weren't you the one who never stopped playing hopscotch in the playground?"

"That's right, and pitch-and-toss too. I was always being told off for playing up the English teacher, old Caillet. Remember him? Every time he chucked me out of his class I'd sneak off to the playground and play hopscotch. That's when you must've seen me."

What a small world! What a strange coincidence! So that was where I had seen him before, at school. He was a senior in the fifth form when I was in the second; we had shared a period in the gym. I remembered him as an uncouth, ill-mannered lout.

He remembered me too.

"Fancy. Who'd have thought we'd meet up in here, eh? We're a couple of school-mate gaolbirds, then. Well, you haven't changed much, you know."

"Nor have you."

I prevented myself from adding, "You're still the nasty piece of work you always were."

Then an extraordinary change came over him. He became unusually silent and pensive. He started to sweat, and looked up at me with embarrassment in his eyes, wringing his hands and muttering distractedly.

Lucien gaped at him. "You having a fit or something?"

[93]

"What a lousy, low-down son of a bitch I am to rat on a school friend. I feel so ashamed of myself. I'm supposed to report on you, to doublecross a fellow Frenchman, an old pal. What a shit!"

"What did I say, Marc?" interjected Lucien, in his odd Berry accent. "He is an informer. Dead right you're a shit, a lousy little Gestapo stool-pigeon. They sent you in, didn't they?"

"Shut up, it's nothing to do with you. I'm talking to my friend here from Saint-Germain. The Gestapo said you were a dangerous terrorist, a saboteur and a spy. They told me to make you talk, and promised to let me go if you did. I was frightened for Denise. They might arrest her and use her to blackmail me. You don't know what they're capable of."

"Oh, don't I? I have first-hand experience of what they can do. Why do you think my face is black and blue and my wrists half paralysed? Did you think I came round here for a drink? If the Gestapo couldn't get me to talk, a miserable little sod like you isn't likely to succeed. So relax. In any case, there's nothing to say."

I felt quite sick. But I was almost sorry for him. I could no longer hate with conviction. The Franciscan had changed me.

He seemed really sorry and crestfallen. "I swear by Denise that it's the first time. I was so scared they might hurt her. She's only a kid, you know. I've never given anyone away in my life. I won't tell them a bloody thing, I swear I won't. They can do what they like to me, but I won't say a word. I couldn't do anything like that to an old friend."

Lucien was a simple man and he expressed his repulsion in his usual blunt way. "I'm no Resistance hero. When I stole from the Boche it was for my own selfish reasons. But you're just a swine. You'd sell your own bloody grandmother if you had the chance. I know that collaborators are always doing the dirty on someone but they have their reasons. They're bad enough, but you'd turn in a pal, you lousy pimp."

Jean N. received this volley of insults with bowed head. He went limp. We saw him in his true colours: a pathetic little small-time crook. He was almost crawling at my feet to ask my forgiveness. He was trembling.

OF BOURGES

"Get to your bed, you louse," ordered Lucien. "We won't talk to you any more, that's for sure. We don't even want to know you're here. You make us sick."

Jean N. did not sleep well that night. He wriggled and writhed on his bed like an eel. His face was drawn and his eyes bleary the next day. Lucien and I ignored him. But it was difficult to send someone to Coventry when we were all shut up together, sharing an eight-by-six room cluttered with mattresses. Jean N. did all he could to redeem himself. He offered me a clean shirt in place of the blood-caked rag that hung from my shoulders. He shared his food with us. He lent us his razor and his newspapers. We learnt from a local newspaper that the Allies had just landed at Anzio. Lucien was overjoyed. "This is the beginning of the end. We'll be free a month from now."

I thought that was rather too optimistic. It occurred to me that if Jean N. was on good terms with the Gestapo we might as well take advantage of the situation. "When the Gestapo talked you into coming in here did they say anything about my cousin Claude Delescure?"

"Yes, they said he was a public enemy and had to be found at all costs."

"They haven't got him then. That's a relief. Thanks. That's all I wanted to know."

Alfred came later that day. He immediately smelt a rat and ignored Jean N.'s ingratiating overtures.

"Watch it, Marc, he's been planted," he whispered to me.

"Yes, I know. He's told us about it. He won't give any trouble."

Five monotonous days followed. We had coffee at seven, then Lucien, who had resigned himself to sharing his life with our informer, played cards with him. They would interrupt their game to have their soup at eleven. Then they resumed again till we went off to take our exercise. After our evening coffee and dry bread "Trousuntshoose" conducted his nightly ritual, and then the lights went out. The last event of the day was Alfred's visit.

The Franciscan still refused to recognize Jean N.'s existence, but I had some long conversations with him. He was no fool. It was a shame he had gone bad.

On September 28th, when we returned to the cell from taking
our exercise, we found two boys there. Serge was a small, fair-
haired sixteen-year-old with rosy cheeks and a young, open
smile. His cousin Jean-Pierre was a lean and lanky seventeen
who wore his hair short and had that dull complexion of the
growing teenager. He was the leader of the pair, though they
were both still kids really, and it was he who told us their strange
story. "We're orphans, you see. We were living with our granny at
l'Hay-les-Roses, working as apprentices. We got fed up with
Paris, though, there was never enough to eat. On August 15th
Gran sent us off on holiday to an uncle in Limoges. He always
had plenty of grub. But when we got to his place he wasn't there.
He'd gone off to join the Resistance, so we got ourselves a couple
of bikes and joined him in the Haute Vienne. It was an FTP
maquis with a lot of commies.[1] We stayed for a bit. It was quite
fun at first. The parachutes would drop out of the air and we
would rush around the countryside picking up the containers.
Sometimes they'd get all caught up in the chestnut-trees and
we'd climb up and disentangle them. We did a lot of shooting
and cross-country marching at night. We threw hand-grenades,
but I liked the tommy-gun myself. The grub was pretty bad,
though, the soup was always cold, and the locals started grumb-
ling about the number of calves we were requisitioning. Then it
rained all the time and there weren't enough blankets. We spent
most of our nights on duty. We had to do all the dirty work
because we were the last to arrive.

"Well, we put our heads together and decided we were better
off at Gran's. Then just before we left I picked up a grenade
and put it in my bag as a souvenir. There was a French policeman at the Vierzon barrier. He looked a decent sort of bloke, so
I said to him, 'We've got something the Boche shouldn't see.
Can you keep it for us?' And he said, 'What is it, food?' 'No,
a grenade,' I said. 'Are you mad?' he said. 'The damned thing
could go off any time. Give it to me. I'll hide it for you.'

"Everything seemed to be fine, but when we got to the German checkpoint what did we see but our grenade sitting there on
the table next to the French policeman, who pointed to us and
said, 'That's them. Those are our boys.'

[1] See Translators' Notes, p. 173.

"So the Boche copped us and carted us off with two fellows they nabbed at the Spanish frontier."

Jean N., Lucien, and I all exclaimed, "The bloody bastard." He must have been a really nasty individual. It was a vile thing to do to a couple of boys.

"I hope you got his number," said Lucien.

"It all happened so fast and we were so surprised that we didn't even think of it. We thought we could trust him, being French and all that."

Jean-Pierre seemed inconvenienced by his detention, but he was not particularly upset. They were both so naïve, so young and unanxious. All Serge could think of was finding a good dry place and sleeping. Everything else could wait. Our cell, which barely held two, now held five. We were packed in like sardines, head to feet. We three did not get much sleep that night, but Jean-Pierre and Serge snored away contentedly.

They were separated next day. Serge remained and Jean-Pierre was put into a cell on his own three doors away. Then Serge was taken off to be questioned at the rue Michel-de-Bourges. Alfred had gone on leave to Germany, but before he left he urged me to remind Serge not to mention the maquis when he was questioned and to maintain that he had found the grenade by the wayside.

Serge returned that evening with a black eye. The poor kid had not been able to take it. He broke down and wept. Schultz had given him a good crack across the face whereupon he told them everything and a lot of make-believe besides. Jean-Pierre had been made into a Resistance hero. They had blown up railway tracks and derailed trains, and so on. We listened terrified. He did not realize he had dug himself a grave. For him it was all a glorious schoolboy escapade, a Boy Scout adventure.

"What are you two looking at me like that for?" he asked, smiling disarmingly. "It's all right, we're in no danger. We'll all get six months at the most and by that time the English'll have landed. The head of our Resistance group told me so. We'll be free by Christmas."

Another chap with illusions.

He was an intelligent boy with a lively curiosity. In his eyes I was an experienced old-timer, quite the seasoned campaigner, an educated man. He never stopped asking me to tell him about the War, my captivity, the future. He had left school after his elementary certificate but he was well informed and he read a lot, mostly popular weeklies. He wanted to go to evening school and do something better than be an apprentice cabinet-maker. His father had been killed in 1939 in the Warndt Forest and his mother had died two years before. His grandmother was working herself to the bone to bring them up.

When we were walking about the exercise court the next day Jean-Pierre called to him angrily from the adjacent yard, "What in hell's name got into you yesterday? Are you mad? You'll get us shot, you bloody show-off. You know damn' well we never even saw a German in the maquis and as for derailing trains—you must be stark raving mad. Keep your silly mouth shut from now on."

"They roughed me up—"

"Did they hell! They gave you a smack on the face and you go shooting your bloody mouth off. They really thrashed the hell out of me because of your stupid lies. They won't believe me now you've given them that adventure story they call a true confession. We're in one hell of a mess and it's all your blasted fault, you stupid fool."

"For Pete's sake calm down, won't you? What can they do to us anyway? Even if they give us two years, the English'll land in a month's time, so there—"

"Two years! When did you dream that one up? We'll be lucky if we get five. Thank God for the Allies or we'd be finished, I tell you."

The exchange had to end then as we were taken back to our respective cells.

I did not know whether Jean-Pierre had really grasped the severity of their situation. I was worried stiff about them. I could not see them getting off lightly.

Then it was Jean N.'s turn to go off to the rue Michel-de-Bourges. Before he left he swore himself red, white, and blue in the face he would say nothing. I was his friend and that was that. I believed him, but even if he did split on me I had nothing to fear. Anything he could have said would have been pure invention. He was back after lunch all bright-eyed. "It's all over for

[98]

me, boys. They're letting me go. They hardly mentioned you, Marc. I just told them you wouldn't talk. They've confiscated all my things but I couldn't care less, they weren't worth much. I won't ever forget you, you know. I'll send you in food every day, starting from tomorrow."

The odd thing is that he was as good as his word.

October 2nd, 1943

On the way in from the yard I noticed an old gentleman in a long, navy-blue greatcoat. He was climbing the stairs with difficulty and Kurt Michel was pushing him about and calling him "idiot" for being so slow. The man had a distinguished face and a grey moustache and looked as if he might have been a retired army officer.

When Alfred took me to the shower that evening he told me that the old gentleman was General Challes. He had been arrested with his two sons, the eldest of whom, Hubert, had been an officer-cadet with me at Saumur. I had always liked him. He was a lively, gay, witty chap and I asked Alfred to remember me to him.[1]

October 3rd, 1943

We were still the same three in the cell. Serge had become far less cheerful since he had learnt that he and Jean-Pierre were to be court-martialled.

At eight in the morning a warder came to get him with a peremptory "Court martial." He left making light of his departure, "It'll be O.K., you'll see. I'll deny it all and explain that I gave them all that nonsense because they'd knocked me about. Cheerio. See you. Who knows? We might even be free by evening."

Youthful ignorance can really be bliss!

Then an hour later I was called to the prison office. Franz Bild, our silent warder, proffered no explanation.

"Come on now, you're wanted below." That's all he would say.

"What can they want me for, Lucien? Do you think they're going to try me too?"

[1] See Appendices, p. 170.

[99]

"Shouldn't think so. The examining magistrate probably wants to have a look at you. They always cross-examine in a difficult or serious case like yours. They like to appear correct, to give the impression they're sticking to all the rules, you know. The examining magistrate goes over the evidence that the police interrogation has obtained and then he goes over you. But Serge and Jean-Pierre's case is too straightforward to warrant calling the magistrate in, so—"

"Come on, cut the gossip," snapped Franz.

I found Yves downstairs. Lucien was right.

I was ashamed to go before the magistrate looking such a mess. Yves looked even worse. We had tatty, dirty beards, long hair, and our clothes were in rags.

We were chained to each other, and two hatchet-faced sentries fell in beside us. I asked them if they could handcuff my sound right wrist to Yves's good arm, but no, they insisted on locking my injured wrist to Yves's paralysed arm. Our two well-drilled military curs unslung their machine-guns and made a great show of clipping on full magazines. They nodded knowingly and warned, "No nonsense or we'll fire. And you're not to exchange a single word, the two of you."

Every security measure possible had been taken to guard our trip. The October sunlight made our eyes smart after the dimness of our cells. They had overestimated our strength. Our legs were very wobbly and moved across the ground slowly. We lagged behind our jackbooted guards.

At one point Yves whispered, "Are they really landing soon?"

I did not have the heart to disillusion him, so I said, "Yes." I no longer believed it myself. Yves was becoming obsessed with the landing dream, like most of the inmates of the Bordiot.

"Shut up," barked one of the guards. "One more sound out of you and I'll shoot your damn' legs off."

Pedestrians who passed us stared at us with pity in their eyes, and I saw one man clench his fists in helpless rage. It seemed miles to the law courts. My legs were getting stiff and I found the going increasingly hard. Yves egged me on and even dragged me by the handcuffs a little.

Just before we got to the Jacques Coeur Palace, at the crossing, we saw a couple of convicts chained together and guarded

[100]

by two soldiers in field grey, a party just like ours, in fact, coming towards us. It was Serge and Jean-Pierre.

"We've just been sentenced to death," they shouted from across the street, and roared with laughter. We must have looked incredulous and startled, for Jean-Pierre confirmed what they had said. "Honestly we have. We've been sentenced to death. But who the hell cares? The English will soon be here and then we'll be free."

Serge raised his free hand and made the 'V-for-Victory' sign, and then the guards pulled them away. That was the last I saw of the poor kids and I will never forget it. Poor wretches! Either they just did not understand or they were putting on an act. Yves went white and I choked. We covered the last few yards to the law courts like a couple of sleepwalkers. That double death sentence filled us with foreboding.

The guards took us up to the first floor where we waited in a corridor. I had been dying to pee ever since we had left the Bordiot, and I could no longer contain myself. This awkward predicament actually saved my life. I asked the guard who had stayed with us while the other had gone to report our arrival to take me to the lavatory. He refused, but I insisted, and he finally consented. He took us both along, Yves still fastened to my side. He pushed us before the lavatory bowl and stood behind us in that confined space, dutifully on guard with the door open behind him. While I was trying to relieve myself he shoved his machine-carbine into my loins. This obviously constricted the flow, so I asked him to be kind enough to undo my handcuffs. The brute refused and started to curse and swear at me loudly, and at that moment a German officer appeared in the corridor.

"What's going on in here? What's all the noise about?" he asked, pointing to us.

"It's these terrorists here."

"Well, undo them, man. They can't pee like that."

"No, sir, I've got my orders. They're dangerous and I'm not taking their handcuffs off nor letting them out of my sight for a single second," replied the guard rather rudely, considering their respective ranks, though admittedly the officer was an army judge and thus not a 'real soldier'.

"Dangerous or not, it's an order," he roared. "I am in charge in these law courts and you'd better not forget it. You will undo those men at once, whether you like it or not."

The guard did so grudgingly. By that time I seemed to have lost all desire to relieve myself.

"Who are you, anyway?" asked the judge.

I gave him a brief outline of our story, much to Yves's amazement, for my brother's German was not as fluent as mine and he had not gathered what was going on.

Then my memory suddenly leapt to our rescue. "Excuse me, but aren't you Major Schleier? Weren't you adjutant to Colonel von Crailsheim in Stalag XIII C at Hammelburg, near Würzburg, in 1941?"

"Yes, why of course, that's it. I thought I'd seen you somewhere before."

What a stroke of luck! Providence had flashed us a smile. It was a chance I could not pass up, and I played it for all it was worth. I told Schleier I remembered him terribly well, though I had, in fact, set eyes on him only two or three times in my life. I chatted about my days as cookhouse interpreter, reminisced, dropped names all over the place, and reminded him of that white Christmas of 1941 in Franconia. I played on his feelings, and brought into bloom that little blue flower that lies in every German's heart.

He softened visibly and Schleier, the military judge, started to call me, "My dear fellow", and said, "Well, come into my office. Let's sit down comfortably and have a chat."

Yves was more and more startled. The guard tried to intervene, but Schleier brought him up sharply.

"You just sit outside there with the brother, and not another word out of you, do you hear?"

Major Schleier was judge and chief prosecutor of the Bourges Military Court. He was a tall, slim, elegant man of about fifty, greying slightly at the temples. He spoke beautifully meticulous aristocratic German, and was dignified and quite imperturbable. He also had that unusual virtue of being an excellent listener. I told him our whole tale, to the very last detail. He shook his head thoughtfully.

"Your brother was mad to have done it, you know."

He had to pay lip service to the usual bits about Bolshevism,

[102]

the defence of Western civilization, and the French and Germans being brothers-in-arms (*sic*), but he did not lay it on very thickly or for very long. It was because, and not in spite of, the fact that I had been a prisoner at a Stalag where he had been stationed that I became a truthful, honest, and innocent man in his eyes. The Gestapo, by contrast, had decided to the contrary and just as quickly. How strangely and how differently do men's minds work!

"Well, my dear chap, it's quite obvious you're innocent. Your cousin Delescure and the English are the guilty parties here. I will have you acquitted and set free. Your brother, unfortunately, has confessed. His is an open and shut case with no loopholes. Caught in the act of spying: Section 3 of the military regulations, which requires the death penalty. There's no way out, I'm afraid. As State Prosecutor it will be my painful duty to conduct the case against him before the military court and demand the death sentence. It's too bad to do this to the brother of a comrade from Hammelburg. It will be a blot on my conscience. It has put me in quite a predicament, and I ask you to believe me when I say I am terribly sorry."

How could I argue? What could I say against his flawlessly logical argument. I pleaded extenuating circumstances, pointing out Yves's youth and idealism, and I stressed the fact that anything Yves might have passed on would have been useless information that the Allies would have known already.

It was of no avail. Schleier had his hands tied by Section 3 of the Code of Criminal Procedure. "The only thing I can try to do for your brother is suggest that the court send on an appeal for clemency to the Führer in Berlin. I can't guarantee its success, mind you. The English are criminals to make young Frenchmen do their dirty work for them. You'll be seeing my colleague Trautmann, the examining magistrate. I'll have a word with him about you. Goodbye, my dear fellow. I've been very moved by our meeting this morning, you know, and regret that it should have been under such painful circumstances."

I emerged from this interview shaking all over. I had to conceal my distress from Yves and—the truth. Before I went into Trautmann's office I whispered to him, "Don't worry. Everything's fine."

[103]

Trautmann was a nice old chap. He was tubby and had a moustache and wore spectacles. It was clear that the Germans were really dragging everyone into active service. He was well over sixty and had obviously been retired a good few years before they had put him into uniform.

"My colleague Schleier informs me you are a friend of his, and he has said much in your favour. Your case isn't too bad in spite of all they've put down in here. We'll see what we can do for you."

He opened a file marked *Tolédano Brothers—Spies*. I recognized my statement, typed by Schultz.

"I should like to make it clear to you that I thoroughly disapprove of the State Security Police's methods. So we will re-examine your case from the very beginning."

He shut the red folder and put it in a drawer.

I then recounted the story again in detail, describing the parts played in it by Claude, Yves, and myself. Trautmann took notes and only interrupted if he wanted something clarified. He ended our interview saying, "Your reason for interceding on your brother's behalf is now clear. Your worries are over. I'll now see your brother and have him confirm your story. Thank you and good day."

How could my worries be over when my brother's life was at stake?

Yves was not in the office long. We set off for the Bordiot again, only this time the guards attached us more considerately, sound wrist to sound arm, and they let us walk back freely and at our own pace. They must have been really impressed by my influential contacts.

I told Yves about the two interviews with the legal officers and of the hope they had given me. I did not say anything about the danger that hung over his head, however, nor did I communicate any of my concern. Yves was not fooled, but he was elated at my prospects and expressed himself in his usual, warm, open-hearted way.

"That's marvellous! I was terrified that something might happen to you and that it would all be my fault. You've been through so much this month, it's about time your luck changed." We embraced at the foot of the staircase and then proceeded to our

[104]

cells. That fraternal embrace said everything there was to say: we loved each other, we respected and admired one another.

I expected to find Serge in the cell, but only Lucien was there, stretched out on his pallet, with tears in his eyes and his face drawn.

"The swines have put Serge into the condemned cell, and the terrible thing is that the kid still doesn't believe it. He shrugs it off, saying it's only a formality because the judges had no choice but to condemn them. He's still confident that they will be pardoned and exchanged for English prisoners, and I don't know what else. He asked me to send you his regards and tell you not to worry. As if you wouldn't! And Alfred's away on leave just when we need him most—"

Before Lucien could finish, in walked Alfred. He had already heard the news. It was written all over his face.

He embraced me warmly. "You see, Marc, you are not alone. God is watching over you."

"Alfred, that won't save Serge and Jean-Pierre."

"Don't twist the knife in the wound. I've just seen them both. They are children and they don't understand. I managed to get them to say a few prayers with me. Serge is quite religious. Jean-Pierre is furious with him. He blames their plight on Serge's extravagant creations."

"I can't make these Resistance blokes out, you know," said Lucien. "There they are in the Haute Vienne playing at being soldiers. They have all the ammunition they need to launch a full-scale attack on the prison here and free us all. At least they'd prove they had some guts. It might be a messy job but they might lift a finger to save their boys."

Alfred did not stay with us long that day. His work as a Good Samaritan had multiplied, for in his absence the Gestapo had filled the cells with cartloads of Resistance men, secret agents, suspects, or hostages, all of whom needed his help as a Franciscan.

[VIII]

Serge and Jean-Pierre were to die. They had finally realized the game was up and that there was no hope of an appeal against their sentence.

Alfred scarcely left their sides for six whole days. His clandestine work as a servant of Christ had taken him to the side of many condemned men during his year at the Bordiot, but he was especially moved by the way Serge prepared himself to face death. The stripling had regained his lost faith. He confided in the Franciscan in his simple way.

"Had I been pardoned and lived I would have become a priest. Thanks to you, Alfred, I know now that it would have been my vocation, that that is what I wanted to do with my life. But before I die I would like to have Jean-Pierre forgive me. I was a coward. I couldn't face the Gestapo and now he has to pay the price of my weakness."

Alfred tried to console him and spoke of Christ's suffering in the Garden of Gethsemane and of Judas's betrayal, and he asked him to forgive the policeman who had given him away not realizing what he was doing. Serge made his last confession and took his last communion quietly and devoutly. Jean-Pierre was not quite as submissive, but he seemed to find some inner peace too.

Serge asked Alfred to lay a wreath on his grave in the neighbouring graveyard after his execution and to tell his grandmother.

"Poor old Gran. She might easily die when she hears. She's taken so much trouble to bring us up and this is the way we thank her. It will be hard on her."

Nothing ever remained secret for long at the Bordiot, and we had a sinking feeling it would happen that night. Lucien was still in a rage. He swore he would batter that policeman's brains out with his wooden leg, and fumed about the useless maquis men who were not coming to the boys' rescue.

"For heaven's sake, Lucien," I reasoned, "be realistic. What could they really do? Suppose they had actually got wind of the boys' arrest up there. You know damn' well the Germans would never let them get within shooting distance of us here."

We did not get much sleep on October 11th. The whole prison waited. We all prayed, even the Germans among us prayed. We did doze off for a spell, but were woken at two in the morning by the revving of car engines. Then the ghastly clank of chains trailing down the stone corridors rang out in the silence. We held our breath, as did Yves in his cell, and as did dozens of political prisoners and dozens of criminals.

The boys' footsteps drew nearer and nearer, past the rows of cells, past the showers, past Cell 84, then Cell 86, and when they were opposite our cell Serge's clear voice rang out, "Goodbye, Marc! Goodbye, Lucien!" Tears involuntarily sprang to my eyes. Lucien made no bones about it. He just burst out crying.

They proceeded slowly down the stairs, their ankle chains dashing against the steps. The clatter that accompanied their departure faded slowly, then was finally gone. The cars had driven off to the firing range where two young French boys were forced to meet their untimely ends because they had trusted a fellow Frenchman.

Alfred fulfilled his promise to Serge. The next morning he went to see his friend and confidant, Férandon, the monumental mason. He asked him to get a magnificent wreath of red carnations and dahlias and arranged to meet him at the cemetery gates. They met and went in, Férandon carrying the wreath. They laid it on the fresh mound that marked Serge's grave and stayed there praying silently for some time. Alfred had not realized he could be seen from the prison, however, and a sentry saw him and reported him to the captain in charge of the guard. The captain sent for Alfred.

"I should like to know what you think you were doing in the cemetery with a civilian carrying a wreath. Were you laying the wreath on the grave of the prisoner who has just been shot? You know perfectly well that this sort of thing is absolutely forbidden. I shall have to punish you very severely."

But Alfred was wily and kept very cool. "But I go to the cemetery every day to pray," he said.

"What's that? You go every day?"

"Yes, of course. Isn't a cemetery the quietest place on earth to pray for the dead, for all the dead everywhere? Besides, part of the cemetery has been set aside for German pilots shot down over Bourges. Fifteen pilots are laid to rest there and I go to pray for them. If I didn't go, who would? Their families are so far away. As for the civilian, I have no idea who he was. He just happened to be there during my visit. I didn't even see which grave he went to."

He told his pious white lies with such quiet conviction that the captain dismissed him, quite convinced of his innocence.

Alfred told me the tale himself the following day.

October 17th, 1943

Lucien was summoned to the court. He was glad to go, for he was fed up with all the uncertainty of his position and not knowing what the future held in store for him. He welcomed the prospect of some change.

"They gave me two years. I'm off tomorrow to Germany to work out my time in one of their so-called rehabilitation camps. But I'd rather go than rot here. Might even get a chance to see a bit of the world. I felt like telling them where they could stuff their two years, mind. The war'll soon be over, anyway."

Saying goodbye after sharing such an eventful and emotionally wearing month was moving and difficult.[1]

October 18th, 1943

I was alone again. Alfred was officially on guard that night. That is, he was not standing in for some truant guard. He was in full charge of the prison, responsible for the maintenance of order and discipline, which proved that his superiors still trusted him.

He came into my cell at about two in the morning. He was not

[1] Lucien Tessier was not to know he was going to the death camp at Neuengamme, where a year later he succumbed to typhus and died. It is a bitter irony that a man should die at twenty-three because a mole had once persisted in devouring his lettuces.

alone, but as he had only coughed once I was not alarmed. He was with the famous Ruetsch, about whom I had heard a good deal. He turned out to be a very pleasant man from Alsace, and I was glad of the opportunity of meeting him.

They were both in a state. The Gestapo had just brought in a hundred prisoners. They had arrived by the lorryload, having been arrested by the military police at Vierzon. It was a somewhat unusual consignment: a whole wedding party, including the bride and groom. After downing a generous amount of Sancerre, the party proceeded to paint the town red way past the curfew, with the result that they were all rounded up and taken off to gaol.[1]

They had not come to tell me this fantastic tale, however. Ruetsch was sure that they would soon decide what was to happen to me. And to Yves too, unfortunately. Ruetsch did not say too much about Yves's prospects, pretending he did not know what they would do to him, but I was sure he was trying to be discreet in order not to alarm me.

October 21st, 1943

Someone banged on the wall of the cell next to mine. I knocked back on the water pipe. The other fellow then shouted, with his mouth against the pipe, and I heard, "Who's there?"

I replied, "I'm here for spying," thinking that that would travel better than my Spanish name.

He answered, "Henri Magnol, Resistance." And I also thought I caught, "See you tomorrow."

Alfred came in just then. He told me the Magnol story, which demonstrated once again Alfred's incredible Christian charity. François Magnol, Henri's father, owned a large factory in Vierzon and his property was very close to the zone frontier along the Cher. He had been helping the Resistance enormously for months. He and his friends Henri Ribière and Thivrier,[2] a member of the Parlement and Mayor of Commentry, who were both active in the liberation movement, got agents from Free France

[1] All one hundred of them without exception were duly sent to Germany as labour conscripts. What a dismal way to spend one's honeymoon!

[2] M. Thivrier was arrested in October 1943, and was tortured by the Bourges Gestapo, as was his English secretary. He was imprisoned in the Bordiot and then sent to Dachau, where he died.

to England, smuggled mail into the unoccupied zone, and harboured Resistance men. Magnol's country house at Maray, near Vierzon, became a central clearing house for important documents. Papers used for Léon Blum's defence at his Riom trial in August 1940 had been made available through this centre.

François and Henri Magnol were arrested at Vierzon on October 19th, probably having been betrayed by former servants. The father tried to escape but did not get far. He was shot down in a street off the Place de la République by Gestapo machine-guns. Despite a couple of bullets in his leg, a shattered thigh, a severed sciatic nerve, and a shot arm, he was thrown into the Bordiot the same day. His condition became almost critical, so the authorities decided to send him to a hospital in Tours. Alfred was told to take the wounded man to Tours in a taxi. He knew his charge was an important Resistance man and that the Gestapo had practically condemned him to death already, so he made up his mind that he would save Magnol, come what may. He could not think how he would do it, however, so he just left it to chance. He told the taxi-driver to take the road through Menetou-sur-Cher, and then spotted a barn a little way from the village. He stopped the taxi in the seclusion of a narrow lane and carried the wounded man into the barn with the help of the driver, whom he then sent to warn Madame Magnol at her home a mile and a half away. She was somewhat bewildered by the news and could not understand what the strange German could want with her. Despite her misgivings she jumped on her bicycle and rode to the barn, where Alfred met her at the entrance. He tried to explain to her in his halting French what he wanted her to do. She was going to be arrested, he explained, so she should therefore go into hiding and destroy every document in her house. Then, in case she were ever caught, she and her husband should work out their stories and make them match exactly. She was to claim total ignorance of her husband's activities.

Noticing the woman's distress he crossed his Rubicon. "Madame, go with husband. Go. Escape. Monsieur Magnol, escape now."

"No, of course not, it's unthinkable. You would only be arrested and shot."

"No worry. I am small Franciscan. Monsieur Magnol important person. Please, it is God's will. You escape."

Then François Magnol, who had heard the conversation, intervened. "Out of the question," he said. "As an honourable man
I refuse to escape on those terms. Even if I did get away, there is
no guarantee that I wouldn't be caught immediately. They'd
soon pick me up around here, especially in this state. Then two
of us would have to face the firing squad instead of one, and
neither of us will have got anywhere. Thank you, Brother Alfred.
I shall never forget your offer, but I cannot accept it. Take me to
the hospital now and do your duty."

They finally persuaded Alfred. Husband and wife embraced
with despair and sorrow in their hearts, for the last time, then
François Magnol was driven off, uncomplaining, to meet his fate.

At Tours he was put in irons: balls on his feet, and chains
about his wrists. François Magnol waited for death in the small
hospital room reserved for the condemned.[1] When Alfred returned he was in real trouble, having taken two hours longer than
usual for the journey from Bourges to Tours. He managed to
clear himself, however, by claiming that the taxi's wood-gas pro-
ducer had broken down. The taxi actually ran on petrol, but
fortunately for him the Gestapo never checked.

October 23rd, 1943

Trial day. The previous day I had been summoned to the visiting room where I found an interpreter sent by Judge Schleier, who
told me I would be called to the law courts at nine the next day.
I would be able to go *unescorted* to hear a formal withdrawal of
my case, but would then have to stay on for Yves's trial as a witness. The interpreter rather gushingly offered me his congratula-
tions, which I didn't really appreciate. I was not overcome with

---

[1] Fortunately the François Magnol story had a happy ending. Madame
Magnol saved his life with her energy, courage, and perseverance. She
managed to persuade a French surgeon to operate on her husband, and
arranged for important people to intervene on her husband's behalf. He
was finally set free. Alfred helped the family immensely. He made it possible for the father to see his son when they were both in gaol, and brought
them food and mail. He even smuggled Madame Magnol into prison
during a visiting period. He hid her in a cell and with a broom in her hand
to make her look like a female prisoner. Then he brought her husband to her
and left them together for a good while.

joy at the news, for Yves's fate still hung in the balance. I was very afraid for him.

When the time came for me to leave the prison Alfred appeared and gave me a great hug. He was very moved and his great St Bernard eyes filled with tears.

"When you go I shall have lost my best friend," he sighed.

"I shall miss you too. If it hadn't been for you, you know, I don't know what would have happened to me. I shall never forget how much Yves and I owe you, how much everyone here owes you. We won't forget when the War is over, and I won't be the last to speak up for you. Most of all, though, I shall always remember the way you helped young Serge meet his end. I need scarcely ask you to take care of Yves as you have cared for me."

He accompanied me to the prison gates where Paul, Gustav, and Franz were waiting to shake hands with me. I left the Bordiot as I had come—empty-handed and desperate.

A military policeman showed me into the courtroom. After a few minutes, in came three members of the military tribunal: Schleier first, accompanied by a clerk and an interpreter, then Judge Trautmann, and finally a jolly, red-faced man who looked like a wine merchant. They wore their uniforms and their decorations. Schleier rose and sped through the reasons that led to the decision not to proceed against me. The interpreter translated, though not very competently: "Whereas there has been no proof that the accused was at any time engaged in any plot against the German Army of Occupation, and whereas there has been no proof that the said accused was engaged in espionage, and whereas there has been no proof that the said accused was the head of any terrorist network, and after thorough examination of all the evidence by the Chief Prosecutor of the Military Tribunal of the Occupying Forces in Bourges, this court in session on this day hereby gives the said accused the benefit of such inconclusive evidence and hereby acquits and releases the said accused from any further proceedings."

Then Schleier added, "This does not mean that we shall not keep an eye on you. You are hereby warned that if you should at any time attempt any illegal act or in any way demonstrate hostility towards the occupying forces, you will immediately be detained and brought before this court which will not show you any clemency."

My freedom was thus to be provisional and probational.

"Next case," said the Prosecutor. "Guards, bring in the brother."

Yves came in, handcuffed, between two military policemen wearing those silly chain dog-collars.

A fourth military judge came in to complete the bench. He was a handsome man with a pleasant smile, and wore a large signet ring which he twisted incessantly.

"Ask Maître Mouquin of the Paris Bar to come in," ordered Schleier.

A lawyer! My parents must have briefed him. I did not know that a French prisoner being tried by a German military tribunal was allowed the services of a French lawyer. They were really playing fair and sticking to the rules. The court, of course, was under ordinary Wehrmacht jurisdiction and in no way controlled by the Gestapo or the SS.

The other unusual feature was that the prosecutor also acted as presiding judge. He personally conducted the case; he summed up against the accused; he pronounced the verdict and passed sentence. His assessors on the bench seemed dispensable, if not useless. The accused was hardly examined at all, the case being largely a monologue conducted by the prosecutor. The accused was reduced to monosyllabic interjections: he could give a yea or a nay and no more.

Schleier's opening speech was quite impressive. "Your worships, in all my years as State Prosecutor I have never before been in the invidious position that circumstances have conspired to place me in today. The case before you is not an ordinary one. The accused is the brother of the man you have just acquitted, and yet I shall shortly be obliged to plead against the brother of a person once confined to a camp where I was adjutant and whom I learnt to respect. The accused is, furthermore, the son of a distinguished professor and writer, a former senior international civil servant. There is nothing to indicate that anything in his upbringing, condition, or family background could have predisposed him to take to espionage and to the wilful contravention of Section 3 of the Army Act of the German Forces in the Field.

[113]

"It is thus with a heavy heart and considerable sorrow that I conduct this case. I can assure your worships that I should have gladly declined this distasteful task had I not felt duty bound not to do so."

Schleier's voice wavered with genuine sincerity. The signet-ringed judge took notes. The other two assessors cleared their throats. The military policemen stiffened with interest at this unusual procedure. Yves, in the dock, showed no sign of emotion.

"We shall proceed with the examination. Prisoner at the bar, stand up," said Schleier.

Yves stood to attention as did the military policemen.

"Prisoner at the bar, do you admit to going of your own free will to Avord and on to the German military airfield there?"

"I do."

"Do you also admit to going with the intention of spying?"

"I do."

"Do you admit that the mission you were on was given you by your cousin Delescure, who had received the brief direct from British Military Intelligence?"

"Yes, I do."

"Will you also admit that the information you collected was to be transmitted by the same Delescure to the aforementioned British Military Intelligence?"

"Yes."

"Do you then admit that your intention was to cause harm to the German Army of Occupation?"

"I do."

"May it please your worships to note that the defendant's replies leave no room for doubt or speculation. We have before us a clear-cut espionage case as ruled by Section 3, which carries the death sentence."

Judge Schleier then proceeded to read his assessors the terribly brief and direct text of Section 3.

"I have a question I should like to put to the defendant," said the nice-looking judge. (I was later to learn that he was an Austrian count, an Anti-Nazi and a Francophile). "The defendant must now regret his irresponsible behaviour. I hope he will give us this assurance."

[114]

The officer was throwing Yves a lifeline. Yves hesitated. Then I think I caught him winking almost imperceptibly at me, and he said in a loud, clear voice, "Yes, I do." In fact what he was about to say and what I feared he would continue to say was, "Yes, I do regret it because I failed and was foolish enough to get caught instead." But that sort of courage would have been not only silly but suicidal.

"I will now call the counsel for the defence, Maître Mouquin."

Maître Mouquin was a very well-known barrister who had some measure of success in German courts and was respected by German judges. His German was fluent. This case was, however, already lost to him. He could not reverse the judgment which everyone knew would be passed. Section 3 had no legal loopholes. All Maître Mouquin could do was engage in a formal legal skirmish.

He began by stressing Yves's heroism, citing the May 1940 incident which happened when he was a mere twenty-year-old. He spoke of our father, described his life-long engagement in international affairs of state, his efforts to bring nations, especially France and Germany, to a closer understanding. He told the court that Yves was the grandson (actually he was the great-grandson) of Frédéric Passy, the first winner of the Nobel Peace Prize. He quoted St Thomas Aquinas, St Augustine, Confucius, and Gandhi.

Having dealt with the moral and human aspects of the case, he got down to Yves himself.

"Let us now examine the facts of the case. When I first looked at this brief—which was only this morning, I might add, before and since when I have not had an opportunity to make contact with my client, who has till this moment been unaware both of my existence and of my appointment to represent him—when, as I said, I looked into this case I was surprised to find so little tangible evidence. The only piece of evidence, the one exhibit, is a small oblong scrap of crumpled paper about the size of a visiting card. On this scrap the defendant was supposed to have reproduced the plan of the entire Avord aerodrome. All I managed to make out was four parallel lines and three small circles. That is all, and it is not much. Your worships, I do beg that we be sensible. If this crude sketch is supposed to represent accurately

[115]

all the complexities of an aerodrome, all its planes, defence
systems, fuel deposits, runways, and so on, then I think we can
safely conclude that British Military Intelligence would have
gained little from such useless information. Nothing will convince me that the English would rely on such nonsense. The
whole thing is quite juvenile. It is scarcely material for two-
penny spy novels—even schoolboys would scoff at its inclusion in
their comic books. It certainly does not warrant or merit the
quantity or quality of attention given to it here by responsible
people like yourselves. Moreover, I read on and found that the
defendant first claimed it to be the plan of a basketball court.
Now, this strikes me as being quite as valid, if not more credible,
as the explanation put forward here. Consider for a moment how
hard it would be to draw a basketball court on a two-by-three-
inch piece of paper; consider how much harder, how well-nigh
impossible, it must be to get a whole airfield the size of Avord
on to the same area. I shall, of course, be brought up sharply and
told that the defendant has already admitted that the . . . er . . .
sketch was, in fact, of Avord. But, your worships, we all know that
every police force in the world has its own peculiar ways of . . .
persuasion. In the light of this common knowledge we can
imagine that an inexperienced, panic-stricken young man might
be persuaded to confess to any manner of things suggested to
him at such a time."

I looked towards the bench to study their reactions. I noticed
a faint smile flicker across the Austrian judge's mouth. Trautmann's eyes met mine for a split second at this reminder of
what he had said about the Gestapo's methods.

"Let us for the sake of argument admit for a moment that
this was a plan of the airfield. Well, in the first place, the sketch
never left my client's pocket, nor was it ever handed on to
Delescure, nor did the English ever get it. Secondly, it is no
slight on the efficiency of the fighters and anti-aircraft batteries to
say that Allied Intelligence already possesses detailed aerial photographs of Avord. This has direct bearing on the honourable prosecutor's fifth question to my client, 'Did he then admit that his
intention was to cause harm to the German Army of Occupation?' This is the crux of the whole case and I claim and maintain
that this is totally inadmissible. I would ask you, gentlemen,

where would we ever draw the line if we started penalizing people for their intentions?"

Maître Mouquin then proceeded to construct a different edifice out of the facts at hand. I was not sure that his picture was very convincing but it seemed to impress the court. Claude became an evil genius spurring Yves on to acts of rash daring. Yves became a guileless simpleton blindly undertaking his cousin's projects. The entire blame was loaded on to Claude's safe shoulders. Claude was, after all, in hiding and unlikely to be caught.

Maître Mouquin wound up by pleading to the judges by calling upon their personal experience of the world, appealing to their feelings and sense of justice. "Your worships, I shall now conclude my defence. I am sure that you, as I, have sons of the accused's age. I would ask you to think of your sons in a similar dock, facing a similar court, answering for acts committed in a similar vein, inspired by identical idealistic convictions, before you decide this boy's fate. I beg that you reflect and reconsider your decision so that you may never live to regret sending the grandson of Frédéric Passy, apostle of peace, to his death on a firing range."

Schleier's voice broke with emotion when he rose to make his final speech for the prosecution. "Your worships, the dreaded moment I spoke of earlier has come. I would like to assure you, sir, that your defence would indeed have convinced and moved any other tribunal, and civil court, to show clemency. But we here are regulated by Section 3 of the Army Act, an Act which is our gospel. Section 3 is uncompromising and absolute. It makes no allowances for extenuating circumstances and interpretations. I should be lacking in my duty if I did not command its strict observance.

"Thus on my heart and conscience be it. We have been torn and moved by this case and by the knowledge that the accused's family is so honourable and distinguished, a family which has fought for peace and humanity. Nonetheless [here Schleier had to pause, for the words simply would not come out] I must ask you to condemn Yves Tolédano to be shot."

The final pronouncement was scarcely audible. Two tears ran down the Austrian judge's face. Trautmann bit his lip. The fourth judge buried his head between his hands and appeared to be praying. Even the two military policemen had been shaken and were sniffling noisily. Only Yves remained unmoved, though he was a shade paler than usual, and seemed to be on the point of consoling his two tearful guardian angels.

Schleier pulled himself together and said, "Prisoner at the bar, have you anything to say?"

Yves slowly rose to his feet, his arms on the edge of the dock, looked Schleier in the eye, and said firmly, " What I did I did for an ideal. I have nothing more to say. Vive la France!"

"Gentlemen," said the prosecutor, "the military court will now adjourn to consider its verdict."

They were out for precisely four minutes. Everyone rose when the judges returned and remained standing.

"Whereas the accused has confessed to the aforementioned crime, and in accordance with Section 3 of the Army Act on criminal procedure in time of war against acts of espionage to the profit of enemies of the state, the prisoner at the bar, Yves Tolédano, is hereby sentenced to death."

"Nevertheless," Schleier hastened to add, "in view of the prisoner's previous record, his youth, and his expression of regret, the court has no objection to an appeal for mercy being lodged and sent to the Führer of the German people, Adolf Hitler. Counsel for the defence, you have forty-eight hours in which to institute the necessary proceedings. The court will rise. Heil Hitler!"

It was all over. The whole trial had lasted fifty-eight minutes. I almost expected the court to turn to Yves and express their regret for having condemned him, such had been the apologetic tenor of the trial. He never flinched for an instant. He even looked relaxed and calm when Schleier pronounced the sentence. The military policemen pulled themselves together, and the four judges left the court looking crestfallen. I went out of a side door hoping to join Yves and his guards in the courtyard when who should I collide with but my parents.

"What happened? What happened?"

"Condemned to death," I murmured.

"Oh, God, no!"

Mother screamed. This tall, self-possessed, handsomely built woman crumpled in my arms. She seemed to shrink and wither, her greying hair turned white, and her eyes dulled. I thought she was passing away and not just passing out. Maître Mouquin rushed to our rescue and tried to bring her round.

"I have just signed the appeal for mercy, Madame. His chances are excellent. The four judges have just assured me that the whole case has been so unusual as to be promising. We must take heart. I have never come across such a degree of dignity and understanding in any other German court, nor such compassionate judges, nor such favourable conditions for mercy."

"Then why have they condemned him to death? Why have they taken my son from me? He nearly died in 1940. It's a miracle that he's still alive. If he had to go, I wish he had gone then."

Schleier fortunately intervened just then. He was most persuasive. "I told Marc how serious his brother's case was and that the outcome was inevitable. I humbly beg that you believe that his chances of being pardoned are heavily in his favour. I have given my entire support to the appeal and the other three judges have also done everything in their power. You can have every hope, Madame. I give you my word as a gentleman and an officer that there is every chance of a reprieve."

Then he added, "I shall see your son in a few moments. I shall instruct the guards to leave you alone with him. You can even accompany him back to the prison. You will be given permission to see him whenever you will. You need only apply to me for a pass and you can rest assured that I shall put myself entirely at your disposal and service. You may rely on me."

Yves soon came out without his handcuffs, escorted at a discreet distance by the two policemen, who were still struggling with their emotions. No-one said anything. One of the policemen finally turned to me respectfully and said, "When you are ready we will move off to the prison. Take your time. We'll hang back a little way."

The situation had changed beyond recognition. It was quite weird. Our strange little procession started off headed by a condemned man walking arm in arm with his parents, followed a dozen yards or so behind by a man who a month ago was regarded as a dangerous terrorist and who now chatted amicably with a couple of embarrassed military policemen. The farewells at the entrance of the Bordiot took some time, but the policemen showed no sign of impatience.

Yves finally left us and the gates closed to behind him. We stood there wondering how long he would remain within those sturdy walls and whether, when he did leave, it might only be on one of those dead-cold, firing-squad dawns.

The return journey by train from Bourges to Saint-Germain-en-Laye was gloomy. Despite Schleier's assurances, none of us felt very hopeful. My father admitted to me—and I could but agree with him—that he laid no store by that bloodthirsty madman Hitler's capacity for clemency. It seemed unlikely that such a maniac would find it in him to pardon a spy at a time when the German armies were suffering great losses and defeat upon defeat, when occupied countries were beginning to reawaken, when ambushes and parachute drops of arms were multiplying, when bombs rained over German towns. That Yves's appeal was supported by an obscure prosecutor from Bourges would, at best, carry no weight. It might actually make matters worse. Reprieves granted by Hitler could be counted on one's fingers. There was no guarantee even that the appeal would reach him. It would probably be slashed to bits by one of those crooked SS dignitaries whose duty it was to isolate the Führer from reality.

Father, on the advice of trusted friends, had made contact with the Resistance. These people had contacts in certain German realms of influence and could obtain Yves's dossier and destroy it and thus ensure that it never reached Berlin. It was a daring scheme, but my father had been assured that these patriots had succeeded before in rescuing condemned men from the jaws of death in this way.

I did not know what to think. I agreed with Father that we should fight to the bitter end, that we would try everything, and, if need be, "dine with the devil himself" if he offered his help.

On October 24th, the day after the crisis, I went downstairs in my pyjamas to have breakfast. It was about eight. My mother had not slept a wink after the nightmarish events of the previous day; she was up and preparing breakfast in the kitchen. Father was still in bed. The gatehouse bell rang loudly and insistently.

The concierge opened the gate and admitted four men in German uniforms. I watched her talking to them and then I saw her pointing in the direction of our house at the top of the garden. I rushed upstairs to hide. The four military policemen knocked and Mother went to open the door.

"We have a warrant for the arrest of a certain Claude Delescure, your nephew, I believe," said the sergeant.

"He's not here," said Mother.

"Well, we'll just search the house, then."

Four pairs of booted feet clumped up the stairs. I hid in a broom cupboard. Officially I had nothing to fear from them, but I was not going to take any risks. There was a lack of communication between the Gestapo and the military police, as there was between Army HQ and the courts, and I had no intention of letting myself be carried off.

They did not search very thoroughly. I overheard the sergeant say to my mother, "I have the other address here: the de Retz farm, near Chambourcy. That's your brother's place, isn't it? Is it far?"

I did not wait for her reply. I had to warn Claude and ward off imminent disaster. Claude was, in fact, lying low at my uncle's house, in bed with a bout of jaundice which seemed to have been brought on by the arrest of Yves and myself. I left my cubby-hole, crept up into the attic, on to the roof (still in my pyjamas), and out on to the neighbouring roof. I banged on the skylight. Our neighbours finally let me in, very surprised to see me, as they had not yet heard I was out of prison. I rushed past them and asked for the phone. There was no time for explanations.

Chambourcy was only five miles away but it was difficult to get through. There was a delay, and I began to get impatient. I was very nervous. Finally, someone lifted the receiver, and Claude's voice came on the line.

"Hello, Claude," I said, trying to control myself and sound relaxed. "Look, Uncle Jules has just been to see us, and he's on his way to you now."

"I see, yes, all right, I've got it," he answered. Then he added in a low voice, "There's someone else here, you know. Your brother Guy is here with a friend."

"What?"

"Guy skipped it and made it to us last night."

At that, I threw prudence and codes to the winds. It was unlikely that they had already started tapping the lines. "Get the hell out of there, all of you," I shouted just before he hung up.

That really *was* the last straw. Guy had escaped[1] and decided to lie low in just the right place: my uncle's totally isolated farm on the edge of the Marly forest. But he was now in danger, and the thought made me shake violently, to the great amazement of our neighbours. They gave me a cup of coffee while I explained briefly what all the fuss was about, and then, still via the roof, I hurried back home.

The police had just left and my mother was assimilating the new shock; I broke the news of Guy's escape and of the danger he was in at present.

It was only in the afternoon that we calmed down when my aunt came round to tell us what had happened that morning.

The four Germans lost their way and wandered around for an hour before finding the place. Very probably the men working in the fields had been asked for directions and had sent the soldiers off on quite the wrong course. They turned up around ten, by which time Claude and Guy had concealed themselves in the thick undergrowth of Marly forest, taking with them plenty of food and warm clothes. They spent the next night in an abandoned gamekeeper's cottage at the source of the Buzot stream.

Claude's and Guy's lucky stars shone for them that morning. The German sergeant happened to be mad about fruit-tree cultivation. He was an expert on apples in particular and owned several acres of Rhineland orchard near Mainz. He no sooner clapped eyes on Uncle's marvellous trees, and on the apples and pears he was picking, than his official mission was forgotten, and he launched into a long discourse on how to treat apple and pear trees. He grew more and more voluble, marvelled at the large, ripe, yellow apples grown from Canadian shoots, compared yields, and tasted the fruit.

My uncle played him along for all he was worth and expressed a lively interest in all he said. He showed him round the chicken

---

[1] He had escaped from a prisoner-of-war camp in Silesia by riding in a wagonload of potatoes, and had arrived in Poissy on the day of Yves's trial.

farm with its incubators and day-old chicks, and took him to see
his milk cows, his horses, and his tractors, keeping him talking for
a good hour. The other three followed their superior with a look
of boredom on their faces, but they seemed quite inured to his
harmless little antics. Conversation then turned to the 1914–18
War, and the two men swapped memories and cavalry tales.

Uncle had not forgotten the object of their visit, however, and
he eventually asked the sergeant, "Well, now, I don't suppose you
came here just to talk about fruit and dairy farming, interesting
though our conversation has been. What have you really come
for?"

The sergeant looked embarrassed. "Er . . . well, you see . . .
we thought your son Claude Delescure was hiding out here. We
have a warrant for his arrest issued by the prosecutor at Bourges."

"Well, in the first place he's not really my son at all, he's my
stepson. And I haven't set eyes on the boy for at least two years.
I sent him packing. He's a lazy, good-for-nothing rascal. I must
say I'm not in the least surprised that he's fallen foul of the
police. I suppose he's been up to some silly prank or other. I
wish you'd trace him and put him behind bars for a bit. He might
learn some sense. I don't really care what happens to him,
frankly."

The sergeant looked relieved and took his leave with a good
deal of heel-clicking and bowing. He did not even search the
place, but thanked my uncle warmly and left him his German
home address and invited him to visit his orchards in the Rhineland once the War was over.

⌈IX⌉

YVES'S DIARY

October 23rd, 1943

I cannot say I was surprised to hear the prosecutor say, "You are condemned to death," this morning. I have made myself get used to the idea over the past fifty-three days and nights. I have schooled myself to be calm. I have become even calmer since going to the examining magistrate. I was at peace when I heard the verdict. A French warder told me that this is peculiar to all criminals and that the greater their crime and punishment the greater their calm. I am not exactly flattered to be in such doubtful company. Are my reactions to identify me with the condemned monster who has clouted an old lady for her meagre savings, with the twisted maniac who has murdered an innocent little child?

This morning in court, as I observed my learned lawyer unfurl his defence with theatrical flourishes of his gown, I had not so much the feeling that I was attending my own trial, but that I was watching someone else's. What brought it all home to me, however, was the sight of Marc's tears when the sentence was passed. I found it hard to grasp that I only had ten days to live, all within the dirty walls of my gloomy old cell. I would continue to vegetate in the stench of the disinfectant exuded from my slop pail, with only fleas for company. It usually takes ten days for an appeal to reach Hitler, be rejected, and return. Ten days is a lot. Poor Jean-Pierre and Serge were shot after six. I will just have time to write the diary of a condemned man. Some diary— twilight scribblings on lavatory paper scratched on with the stub of a pencil that escaped confiscation. I'll jot down some day-to-day impressions, note the passing of time, the passing of identical days. My jottings will bear witness to my mounting fears. They will record what memories come to mind, as well as the lengthen-

ing shadow of death which one early dawn will come and take me
out into the chill darkness. The thing I miss most after my parents
and brothers is music. I shall never hear my mother playing the
piano again, putting so much feeling into Chopin's sonatas, the
notes flowing from her fingers. I often used to ask her to play
something for me, anything she liked, while I curled up on the
sofa, my eyes shut, and let the music carry me away.

Poor Mother, how you will suffer! How will you ever bear my
death if you were so shaken by the news this morning? That
scream I heard was full of love and reproach, a mother's lament
for the loss of her son. That cry hurt me more than the sentence
itself, more than all the beatings. I have caused my loved ones
so much sorrow for so little, for nothing really. I wish I had died
fighting with a gun in my hand. But fate has chosen to depict
me to posterity as some wilful boy who once rushed recklessly to
an ignominious death, an undisciplined, stupid fool cut off at
twenty-four for having failed miserably to do his duty: the anti-
hero of a mission that went wrong. Yet there are some compensations. There is Alfred, whose round, cheery face appeared between the bars of my punishment cell where I lay rotting for
twenty-three endless, dark nights. God must have sent Alfred,
who came smiling with pocketfuls of food. He stood there awkward and self-conscious, his rough uniform bursting over his
generous paunch. But his face through those bars radiated love
and kindness. He came back again and again with messages from
Marc, with letters and parcels from my parents. He never stayed
longer than three minutes in order not to be caught. His smile was
such a welcome change from Gustav's drunken, bleary face, and
from Michel's sadistic scowl which would split sideways into a
nasty smirk as he tightened my chains a notch tighter whenever
I asked him to loosen them a little.

My Franciscan guard would come and smuggle me into a
shower in the dead of night while the prison slept. He spread foul-
smelling ointments on me and gave me tablets, and I always felt a
new man after these visits. Then there was the Abbé Barut incident. I couldn't believe it was all really true and happening at
first. I kept pinching myself. But the priest was really there and
he and Alfred were really laughing their heads off like two long-
lost friends sharing an old joke. Then there was the day when

Alfred came with the civilian prisoners' cook, all dressed up in his chef's tall white hat. The cook came to give me a parcel which he pushed through the bars, and when I asked him who had sent it he answered gruffly, "Never you mind. You've got friends and they care, and that's all."

I'm sure he must have passed the hat round to pay for the parcel. The next day I saw a broom head appear between the planks of my boarded-up window, and impaled on the bristles were three cigarettes and some matches. I was really touched. The fellows who had thought it all out may have been a bunch of crooks, murderers, and thieves, pariahs of society, but as far as they were concerned I was in the hell-hole and they felt for me. Alfred probably told them about me. Alfred spends his whole life thinking of others. What a man is our Franciscan! What a man! He doesn't have to say anything, one just knows he is good. I can't really understand what he says, but those blue eyes of his communicate more than any French he could ever speak or German I might grasp. Yes, there are compensations. Marc's release is one. He came rushing to my rescue only to get himself well-nigh crucified, after he'd already done three years as a prisoner of war. It was wonderful to know that he was cleared and freed, thanks to the help of a German officer.

It is also a consolation to know that one is not abandoned, not alone, that Father is battling away for me, that Alfred and all my friends around me are pulling for me. I am sure that few are so fortunate and that many here in Bourges and elsewhere are left to their own devices and die hopeless and alone.

One is never alone. There is always God. There is prayer and it is a great strength and help. Every day, and then at night when the cold and my own despair keep me awake in my dungeon, I pray for Marc, for my mother and father, for all the men in the other cells, for all the nameless sufferers everywhere. That very simple faith my parents gave me has helped me withstand these trials. God bless you, Mother and Father, and Marc and Guy, may He give me the strength to persevere and hold out until my execution. I don't think I am afraid of death. It is this dreadful waiting and the uncertainty that goes with it that wears me down. Oh, God, please let me live, let it not all be ended so soon. I still want to live.

[126]

October 24th

I've been allowed to take some exercise, but while all the other prisoners walk round one way I have to walk in the opposite direction. They must still think I am dangerous. I end up in the women's section and find myself alone for half an hour in a triangular court, two sides of which were about ten yards long, and the other about five. A window above the courtyard flew open today and two boys leant out and asked, "What the hell are you doing out there?"

"Exercising. How about you up there?"

"We're peeling spuds."

"How long have you got?"

"Two years. We got caught breaking into a supermarket. Didn't you read about us in the Châteauroux papers? What are you here for?"

"Spying."

"You're in the German part, then? Been tried yet?"

"Yes."

"What'd they give you?"

"Death."

"You're joking."

"No, I'm not."

"Hell, you certainly don't look like someone facing a death sentence. What are you so cheery about?"

Perhaps it was Alfred's pills that made me look bright and cheerful. He came into my cell last night and gave me two sleeping pills, but I don't think I really needed them as I was dead beat after that long walk. I am not used to moving about much any more.

Sunday, October 26th

I am still haunted by music. Last night I dreamt I was at a concert. The orchestra was at least a hundred strong and they were playing Beethoven's *Eroica*, a masterly rendering of the dialogue between the brass and the strings. I dreamt every single note. It was quite extraordinary. The cracked prison bell woke me up at seven o'clock.

I can't understand how I could have dreamt the whole symphony when I can hum no more than a dozen notes of it. I heard every instrument come in exactly as it should. I told Alfred and he said he thought it was a gift from God.

Monday, October 27th

I shall describe my warders.

The staff sergeant-major: A good-looking chap with grey hair worn in a crew-cut. He's pleasant enough but a stickler for rules and regulations.

Paul: About forty-five with a rugged face, not a bad chap, really.

Franz: Small, weasel-like face with sunken eyes behind rimless glasses. He came into my cell this morning and complained that it wasn't clean, yet I swill it out every day, for lack of anything better to do.

Ludwig: Looks a complete fool. Not bad.

Gustav: Great lout of a chap with a sprout for a nose. He's the only corporal, all the others are warrant officers. He seems to have an enormous weakness for girls and for drink, and appears not to worry about anything else.

Kurt Michel: A real bruiser. He kicks, clouts, shoves, the lot. He never talks, but shouts all the time. His French isn't bad. A perfect Gestapo type.

Alfred: He is, of course, a warder, since he goes on duty and also supervises some of the exercise periods. Alfred is what Providence would look like in uniform. When he holds me I experience the same sensation of comfort and ease that I did when they used to change the dressing on my wound and it hurt, so that I would bury my face in the bosom of some buxom nurse who smelt of soap and ether. That always seemed to take away the pain.

[X]

Mother and I took advantage of Schleier's offer to let us visit Yves at Bourges.

My heart skipped a beat when we stepped into Schleier's office. It was October 28th, five days after the trial. The prosecutor greeted us warmly and again repeated his assurances concerning Yves's pardon, but I no longer trusted anyone's assurances. I had learnt to be wary. We both wondered whether we should even find my brother alive. Alfred was waiting for us at the gates and his smile reassured us. He went to fetch Yves, who looked much better; his colour was returning and he had put on a little weight. In veiled language I told him of Guy's escape, and his face lit up with joy.

It was wonderful to talk to him, despite the interpreter's presence, and he seemed to be in excellent spirits. "I've everything I need," he said. "I'm waited on hand and foot and I owe it all, of course, to Alfred. It's incredible how much he does around here."

Yves said he was convinced he would be reprieved and I couldn't help admiring his optimism. Mother managed to hold back her tears. When we left Yves we were both chilled by the same idea. What if that were the last time we saw Yves alive? Suppose they shot him before we came next week when the normal ten-day period was up!

Alfred was waiting for us in the courtyard and told us to take heart. A French warder opened the main door and who should I bump into but Ernst Basedow! He was going into the Bordiot alone, looking as florid and bloated as ever, a leather briefcase under his arm. The colour drained from my mother's face when she heard him bellow, "What do you think you're doing? You free? Why haven't they shot you? Who let you go? You just wait, you bloody little terrorist. I'll fix you yet. You won't get away this time." Whereupon he charged into the prison.

[129]

I took to my heels and ran for life. I took a short cut round the prison and rushed on to the railway footbridge, leaping up four steps at a time. I dashed into the waiting-room, then, dizzy and panting, I joined the crowd round the ticket office and hid behind a pillar, shaking like a leaf. Basedow had revived all the memories I had tried to suppress. Mother soon joined me, looking pale and drawn. Ernst had not come out of the prison, so he might have been bluffing, but we took no chances and caught the first train to Tours rather than wait for the Paris express. We got home without any further trouble but we were both upset by the incident, which had marred the pleasure of seeing Yves.

The next day I woke at six, and decided to do so every day. The previous day's fright and the recent visit by the military police made me extremely cautious. If I were constantly on my guard I would have the advantage of advance warning and could then escape over the roof. Father now left the house every morning at dawn, to go to Vichy, to the Swiss Embassy, to the lawyer, and to secret meetings with the Resistance.

"We're nearly there," he would say. "I think we're on the right track now."

I stayed with Mother all day long, as I did not want to leave her alone, and kept a sharp eye on the gatehouse all the time. We ate our scanty meals together and never stopped thinking of Yves in his cell in the Bordiot. The waiting was intolerable and, though friends came to try to cheer us up we remained a dreary pair.

I got wind of a printer in the town who had an influential German contact, an SS officer or senior Gestapo official who was the printer's drinking mate. I called on the printer, and was confronted with a toothless drunkard suffering from acute cirrhosis of the liver, about sixty years old and purple in the face. He was pleased I had come and anxious to do something to help clear himself. I also gathered that his German friend was eager for an opportunity to cover his position in case things turned out badly for his country. Between swigs of Pernod the printer told me that the time was ripe for such a deed and that I need worry no longer about my brother. I almost believed him.

That evening Father came home looking haggard and tired. The lawyer had suddenly become pessimistic. He feared the worst and foresaw a rejection of the appeal. News from the Russian front was bad—the Red Army had just launched its great winter offensive. The Allies had also intensified the bombing of Germany, and the Germans were getting frantic.

"Well, that's a dead end. We must approach the problem from a different angle. I've worked something out with the Resistance people and we must hope it works before it is too late."

On the ninth day hope came to us at last.

"They've done it, by Jove. They've got hold of the dossier and destroyed it." Father beamed happily.

Through his friend B. Father had made contact with a Parisian society woman. We never knew her name. B. always referred to her as "the person". She served his Resistance group by 'seducing' certain senior German officers, usually Gestapo men, with sums of money. Many Germans were really living it up in the capital and getting badly into debt. They kept chorus-girls, they were well stocked with luxuries from the black market, and they spent weekends in the country, all of which cost a considerable amount of money. Whatever they agreed to do they did for money, and not for politics or ideologies or out of any apprehension as to their future standing. Their motives, as their lives, were totally corrupt. All they seemed to want was a never-ending merry-go-round of varied pleasures and they were prepared to pay for it. They had to be flattered and humoured, their confidence had to be bought and won. Dinners and parties were held in their honour, in the course of which they would be slipped envelopes "for Nazi Party charities." This was the job of the lady in question, and when her delighted guests were well in their cups and glowing vaingloriously amid these contrived festivities she could be handed some vital dossier which could save a Frenchman's life.

Needless to say, it cost my father a small fortune. Yves's case was a serious one and the SS contact played for the dangerously little time we had and pushed his price up. Twenty-four hours before the statutory delay was due to expire, he delivered the dossier to "the person", who promptly threw it on the fire. The same Gestapo officer issued discreet orders to Bourges that Yves should remain a prisoner but that no further action should be taken. The file had been 'officially' burnt during a Berlin air-raid. The Reich Chancellery had, in fact, recently been hit during an Allied air-raid, so the story was plausible.

Yves's position in prison was a strange one. He was a condemned man but with no dossier, mysteriously protected, a 'floating' prisoner, but who had not been officially reprieved. Had he been reprieved he would have been sent off to a hard-labour camp, to Dora, or Buchenwald, or to the salt mines.

"He's safe," cried Father. "It's like waking from a terrible nightmare. Now we've got to get him out of the Bordiot."

Although Mother and I were relieved that those nine ghastly, almost sleepless, days and nights were over, we did not fully share my father's joy, and were not even cheered very much. The Basedow incident had made us both wary and fearful.

"Oh, I shall never be able to forget those awful eyes, and that perfectly loathsome face," my mother kept saying.

What really worried her was that Yves's present protection could come to an abrupt end. His continued existence depended on the whimsical good will of a blackmailer. The bastard could threaten to change his mind and issue new orders if we did not give more money. "I know," said Father. "It was a calculated risk but it was our only chance. If he does we'll just have to meet his price. I'll borrow the money. I'll sell the shirt off my back if need be. It's either that or the firing squad."

I kept quiet. I knew what Yves and I had been through at the hands of the Gestapo. I knew what others had been forced to endure in the rue Michel-de-Bourges. I had learnt a lot in prison. I remembered the men who had been shot during my forty-five days in the Bordiot. I knew that Yves's life was in constant peril, and I trembled for his safety. When Father insisted that Yves's case was closed, that he was not in the Gestapo's hands, I knew him to be wrong. The Gestapo could do anything they wanted. If they chose to get rid of Yves they would do so. They would not be stopped by any amount of orders from a member of their own pack. They had their ways of fixing things. A hungry wolf does not stop to ask if the lambs grazing on the other side of the fence are his or not.

My mother had the same misgivings but neither of us admitted them to the other. I felt happier after I had gone to see the printer the next day. His German had made inquiries and had been informed that Yves's dossier had disappeared and that he was safe in prison. This, at least, confirmed the reports we received from "the person" and from B. It also proved that the printer's friend was well placed and had access to the rue des Saussaies. I realized that there was no point in continuing my association with the printer, but he, on the other hand, was reluctant to discontinue his services. He phoned me three times telling me to come and see him because he had important news, but when I finally went all I got was an earful of drunken nonsense. He drooled all over the place and kept losing his false teeth. I was nauseated by him and all he stood for.

[XI]

YVES'S DIARY

Monday, November 3rd

There was a great commotion last night. Doors slammed, boots thumped all over the place, and chains clanked. Every time I heard footsteps approach my door I held my breath.

Suddenly the key turned in the lock and my light went on. I sat bolt upright. It was only that stupid Ludwig who came in to ask me for some soap. What a relief! I flung the soap at him and told him to bloody well keep it.

However, if it was not my turn, it was for nine other men; a complete Resistance group "done in", as Joseph put it when he brought me my coffee.

Alfred came in during the morning, looking pale and unhappy, his eyes wet and red-rimmed. He clasped me, turned on his heel, and left without a word.

I cried and prayed for them.

Tuesday, November 4th

I am being really spoilt. Mother came from Paris and brought me a pile of food. I never knew I had so many friends. Everyone at Saint-Germain sent me something, like a piece of salami or a cake made with real flour. I insisted that Alfred share the food with me this afternoon, while Pussy had some salami skins at "Kontroll" this evening. Pussy is a dear little black-and-white cat that sleeps by the stove in the guardroom. "Kontroll" is a night round when the warder on duty goes round every hour, switching on the lights in every cell and squinting through the peephole to see if the prisoners are all right. Alfred always comes in for a chat on his first round. He calls me his "great friend" and "my Yves".

[134]

THE FRANCISCAN OF BOURGES

Wednesday, November 5th

My ten days are up and I am still alive.

At eleven o'clock an NCO interpreter from the military court came to tell me that my sentence had been confirmed by Paris HQ, but that my appeal had been sent to Berlin and that the reprieve should soon come through. If it does I shall be sent off to a hard-labour camp for a good ten years. If I survive I'll be thirty-five, but there is always a chance that the Allies might land before then, of course.

Even if I do have to go, I think I'd rather go to a salt mine and work myself to the bone out in the light and the open air than wither in this dark, dank cell.

November 7th

Now the tenth day has passed the idea of death is losing its sting. I am beginning to be more hopeful and see things differently. I shall probably not write my diary every day now. Life goes on. Everything seems calm enough for the moment and yet the prison is never really quiet. It was almost empty a few days ago and now it is full up again. It appears that those who leave here are sent to concentration camps.

I once told Paul that I envied those people. He winced, and whispered hoarsely, "I wouldn't send my worst enemy to the place they go to, mate. Just you pray they keep you here."

He is probably exaggerating.

November 10th

We've got a new interpreter—Sergeant Müller. He looks a decent sort of chap. He is supposed to listen in on our visits but he seems to take little interest in our conversation and frequently slips away. Mother took advantage of one of his long absences to tell me that my appeal never reached Berlin. I don't know how Father managed to have the dossier intercepted, but apparently someone laid hands on it in Paris and burnt it. I don't have a record or a file now and, so to speak, I no longer exist as a condemned man. The people involved in this transaction, the Resistance or anti-Nazi Germans, have even informed the military court here that the dossier was burnt in a Berlin air-raid. That is the official story. The people at Bourges are upset, though, and they have asked my lawyer to compile another dossier. Maître Mouquin is now free to cast all sorts of new light on the case and shove in anything he fancies. How marvellous! I have noticed that for several days they have been treating me with unusual courtesy and consideration which I thought strange considering my death sentence. Bourges must be convinced that I enjoy some sort of mysterious protection in high places, and that there is something strange about my case. What a brilliant coup! My father is a genius, God bless him.

November 13th

I have now been in solitary confinement for seventy-three days and have even started talking to myself of late. This morning, however, I acquired a companion: a dim-witted farm hand who had been caught rifling through the desks of some municipal office with a tommy-gun in his hand. He had worked for the FTP and had then taken to small-time racketeering like the stealing of ration cards. I find it rather hard to hold a conversation with him. When we go out in the courtyard for exercise he keeps saying, "If only I had a tommy-gun, if only I had a tommy-gun." Well, we don't have one. We don't even have a ladies' handbag pistol . . . so there you are, chum. All we have is our thoughts and prayers. It is absolutely pointless even to contemplate breaking out of this place.

Nature has not been generous to this particular son of hers. He is ugly. He is dirty. He smells. He looks like a maltreated mongrel and he snores at night. And to add to all this they went and shaved his head, which hardly improves matters.

November 14th

The poor chap has been condemned to death. Perhaps that is why he is in with me. I am trying to cheer him up and give him some sort of moral support, but it's no use. He doesn't read. He has no spiritual life. He has absolutely no faith. What can bring him peace? How is he going to survive the days of waiting?

November 15th

I am alone again. They've moved him to another cell. I don't

[136]

even know his name. Two other young fellows have been condemned with him.

November 23rd

Wholesale clearance this morning! Nine men, including my recent companion, were shot.

Alfred came in with tears in his eyes. They all faced their ends bravely, he said. My chap went dumb and limp. He even tried to commit suicide.

I reproach myself bitterly for not having been kinder and more patient. He was an orphan. He was alone in the world. No-one will shed a tear for him except Alfred and myself, and we shall soon forget him.

January 8th, 1944

There was one hell of a rumpus at half-past four this morning. Joseph told me it was not an execution but a convoy of convicts setting off for Orleans. They were mostly victims of Paoli, the French collaborator who works with the Gestapo. Among them was a Madame Cherrier whom Paoli had tortured. That beast of a man can't even keep his hands off a woman. The prison was almost empty, but now it has filled up again and they say that Paoli gets worse every day. I have a new neighbour in Cell 98. He used to be in the cell opposite. He's been here since November. As soon as he was moved he rushed over to the "telephone" to tell me his name: Combanaire. He used to own the Terminus Hotel at Montluçon, and was arrested for having a shot-gun in his attic after someone informed on him.[1] He is a very worried man. His wife and daughters come to see him regularly. He's concerned about his business and his family. He has not been sentenced yet, or even come before the military tribunal, but has only experienced the usual Gestapo reception ceremony.

The heating pipe, the "telephone" that runs through all the cells, enables us to communicate fairly well. When we want to

---

[1] M. Combanaire did not tell Yves the whole story. His hotel had been a Resistance arms depot and had also housed a radio transmitter. He was one of the five main local Resistance men, and finally returned alive from one of the death camps.

talk we bang on the pipe for a bit and then start up. I have managed to make contact with prisoners several cells away. We can also pass messages along like this.

January 13th

A general came round on an inspection, and Chief Warrant Officer Bardé brought him to my cell to show him how "well kept" it was, and spoke very highly of me. Alfred hovered in the background, winking furiously. I am now one of the oldest inhabitants of the place and quite the warders' favourite.

Bardé returned to ask me if I wanted to do some work because he had obtained special permission from the General to let me do so. So I am now busily engaged in making pay-packets which I cut out of old maps and stick together with glue. While I work I needn't think, and when I've finished I stretch out on my bed and rest.

January 23rd

I met three young men in the showers, one from Cell 99, who have all been before the tribunal though none of them have been sentenced yet. Alfred is sure they won't be condemned to death. Theirs is a complicated story which is supposed to boil down to finding some grenades on some waste land and then being arrested.

February 19th

The poor fellow from 99 has been sentenced to death. I hope he'll be reprieved. His friend Cogoï has got fifteen years hard labour and is off to Germany.

February 23rd

Combanaire and Thivrier, the deputy for Montluçon who is seventy, were both packed off this morning, but they weren't released. Where did they go? Poor Combanaire thought they'd set him free.

February 24th

We've got a new NCO, who seems quite a nice fellow. He's a hundred times better than that unspeakable creature Michel, gone to the devil knows where, with Alfred's blessing.

[138]

March 1st

It's all over for René in Cell 99, who was shot this morning. Poor chap, he had bad chilblains, but he won't feel the cold now. He won't complain of handcuffs any more, either. A deathly hush always settles over the prison on execution days. I can't make out why some men are tried, sentenced to death, and shot, while others are sent off to Germany, often for much more serious crimes. The ways of the Third Reich are mysterious indeed!

March 10th

Alfred came in ranting and raving. I have never seen him in such a state before. He was furious.

"That swine Paoli is at it again. He's just been at a Resistance group and he's tortured M. Bicyclette[1] beyond the realms of human possibility. I've just come from his cell: he's nothing but a blood-soaked rag. Paoli is a vile, loathsome beast. Someone should riddle him with bullets and be done. He's a psychopathic murderer."

March 14th

Between the two of us we've made five hundred pay-packets today. Yes, I have a new companion. He came in yesterday evening, an enormously likable fellow called Gaston Roy from Clamecy.

He belonged to an FTP Resistance group and was coming home on leave when he and a friend were picked up by a couple of French policemen just as they were coming round the bend of an isolated path. There was no real evidence against them, so they were put into the civilian wing. However, a former member of their group, who had gone off with a machine-gun to get what he could out of local farms and municipal offices, had also been arrested by the Gestapo. This individual saw Gaston and his friend in one of the prison corridors and promptly gave them away in a bid to save his own life, so they are now the responsibility of the Gestapo. The lousy coward told the Gestapo the lot—the whereabouts of the group's headquarters,

---

[1] See Appendices, p. 169.

their arms dumps, the names of the leaders, and so on. This meant that his two victims could not possibly deny the accusations, and so they had no alternative but to sign their statements.

March 20th

Alfred came into our cell this afternoon with a pair of handcuffs to see how I would react. He put them on me and when I asked why he just said "Gestapo". He returned a few minutes later roaring with laughter at his practical joke and at my gullibility. I had gone deathly white and looked quite ill, but this had the happy result of convincing Roy that I was a real prisoner. He had had his doubts about me for my story had struck him as so extraordinary and my relations with the warders so unusually good and friendly that it had occurred to him that I might be an informer.

Thanks to this somewhat clumsy joke my friendship with Gaston has become very much firmer.

March 27th

I am so pleased to be sharing a cell with Gaston. He is intelligent, has an excellent sense of humour, and is always cheerful and in a good mood. We discuss all sorts of serious subjects. We read a lot and then talk about what we've read. Müller, who is a very decent fellow, provides us with reading material. Alfred told me today that it was he who managed to arrange for Gaston to be in with me. He had decided to wait for the arrival of a prisoner who was "a cut above the usual" to put in with me so that we could help each other and not be so lonely. I am very grateful to him for this consideration.

Gaston and I work hard. We still make pay-packets but we now have a sideline making up decks of playing cards. We cut out bits of red and black paper from *Signal*, the pro-German weekly, and then stick the bits on to form the pips. It's all a bit rough and ready, but it seems to please the card enthusiasts and stops us from brooding too much over our fates.

I have been alone now for three consecutive mornings, as they've been taking Gaston off to the examining magistrate, the same one that dealt with Marc and me. He listens patiently to all Gaston has to say and is not too pessimistic about his case. I

think he'll probably get five years in Germany. The more I get
to know Gaston the better I like him. He is a marvellous companion. We have so much in common and we are sharing so
many trials and tribulations that we are now particularly close.

April 4th

Disaster! Alfred is leaving us. He is being transferred to a
prison in Dijon and came in to tell us the sad news this morning.
He's going on a medical refresher course at the Foch Hospital in
Paris first. He's been promoted to the rank of sergeant and is
quite proud of it.

This is a sorry day for us at the Bordiot, but a happy one for
the Dijon prisoners, who will benefit from Alfred's kindness just
as we have done here.

As Alfred points out, we'll still have Müller, who is a sensitive,
perceptive, cultivated, and very understanding man. The other
day I gave him a letter for my parents which I had not sealed, in
accordance with the prison censorship regulations. He refused
to take it, saying gently, "My dear Yves, I am an interpreter,
not an informer. Seal the letter. What you have to say to your
parents is no concern of mine."

Visits are only supposed to last ten minutes, and the interpreter is supposed to be there all the time. When Mother comes
Müller bows and kisses her hand—unheard of courtesies round
here—then proceeds to give her news of my welfare, "Yves is
in good spirits. He's always singing. Everyone in prison likes
him," and so on.

He then leaves us for two hours or more, and never searches
Mother's bag or checks to see what she has given me.

April 8th

Müller stayed chatting with us for ages today. He brought us a
book by André Gide and we discussed literature for a good hour.
Gaston, who left school after his elementary certificate, just sat
and listened to us. Müller told us about himself. He was born in
Würzburg, and has a Ph.D. In civilian life he is a singer at the
Vienna Opera House, and he's travelled about quite a bit,
working in operas in London, Paris, New York, and so on. We
asked him to sing us something and he quietly obliged us with

"La donna è mobile" from *Rigoletto*. He is a very good baritone. He has fine, regular features which aren't typically German at all, and he always looks rather sad. He seems to admire Jews a great deal: "I have never known a Jew to break his word," he told us.

He loathes Nazism and always refers to Hitler as the *Sauhund*.[1] He predicts the fall of Germany by the end of the year and hopes the Allies will land soon.

Talking of Jews, I remember something that Alfred told us a few days before he left.

"Do you know what *they* tried to make me do today? Take a Jewish woman away from her child! 'Give me any other order you like and I'll obey,' I said, 'but that one I shall *never* obey!' They didn't insist."

April 15th

The days fly past in Gaston's company. He is such a nice person and we understand each other perfectly. We seem to have identical tastes, the same sort of feelings and reactions. We sometimes even forget we are in prison. For the first time in ages I am actually happy, and this is the first time I have experienced such a genuine friendship for anyone. I hope and pray he will stay with me for some time yet.

He was never a believer, but we have been reading aloud from the Bible that Mother brought me every evening before going to sleep. We have also been praying together. Gaston has just said, "Thanks to you, Yves, I have found Christ," which touched me deeply.

May 9th

Gaston is to go before the court tomorrow to receive his sentence. They came to tell him this evening. I am praying as hard as I can for him.

Wednesday, May 10th

Gaston, my friend and brother, was condemned to death today. We are so close, we have shared so much. He is going to have to live through the ordeal I underwent six and a half

[1] Literally "Sow hound".

months ago. They took him to the court at eight this morning. All the time he was away I paced up and down the cell like a caged beast, obsessed with the desire that his life be spared.

He returned at noon and fell into my arms with the news. Then Franz took him off to Cell 93. I think my distress is worse even than when I was sentenced. To have found and made such a friend and then to have him wrenched away, to lose him . . . God have mercy on him.

May 11th

I can't sleep. I can't stop crying. I won't eat. I beg for news and cry again. Müller and Paul are also very upset. They bring and take our messages. They tell me that Gaston's morale is extraordinarily high and that he never stops singing. He sends me such cheerful notes. It is *he* who is bolstering *me*!

May 12th

He's a terrific chap. Everyone loves him and all the warders come in to tell me about him. Bardé is convinced he will get off. The judge could hardly read the verdict, he was so upset. I am sure that it was the Gestapo who ordered the sentence, because it is excessive punishment for what he did. His note yesterday was so calm and confident that I can but admire him the more. "I hope I shall be reprieved. If I am not I shall die a noble death. At least I now have the comfort of knowing that we shall meet again, my dear friend. God will not abandon me. I have faith in Him. . . ."

May 13th

The man who betrayed him was shot this morning. He was mistaken in thinking that the sacrifice of his comrades-in-arms would save him. He went to his death a terrified man. It was awful to hear his blood-curdling cries pierce the darkness. What an end! How bitter and guilty he must have felt! May God have mercy on him!

May 14th

Paul arranged for Gaston to come to my cell for a few minutes. I can't bear to think of them shooting him in cold blood.

May 15th

Joy of joys, we met in the showers. Franz arranged for us to go at the same time, although we aren't in adjoining cells.

"I must have a good scrub. Who knows, I may have to meet my Maker at dawn tomorrow," Gaston said to me.

Bardé came specially to tell me that he would put us back in the same cell as soon as possible.

May 16th

At exercise today he was in the next yard. He is as strong and as resolute as ever. It is infectious—I am beginning to think we really may meet up again as free men.

He said in his note today, "I have prayed with such fervour that He is bound to hear my pleas and save me. He is so good. He has given me faith and that is a great thing." When I get depressed I look at the large cross that Gaston pencilled on the wall, and it helps restore my courage.

May 17th

Gaston writes, "I hope Paul will be able to bring you to my cell for a few minutes today. I want you to see my crucifix. I am surprised at myself. I can't draw to save my life and yet I have drawn a well-proportioned Christ. I am sure God helped me. Fortunately Franz, who is such a stickler for the rules, hasn't seen it. He would make me rub it off. I prayed that he shouldn't notice it and I think He must have granted me my wish. Now I have something to say my prayers to. It really does help. When I look at Christ I feel stronger. I think of all He went through and realize how paltry my own sufferings are. He was an innocent man paying for the sins of the world. I am paying for my mistakes. . . ."

Gaston has changed so much. When I first knew him he was given to occasional rebellious outbursts, but then he seemed to learn an inner peace and began to pray. He is a fine example to me.

May 18th

I have had a long letter from Gaston, full of hope and faith. He told me that some charming gentlemen from the Gestapo came to see him and showed him some photographs of three boys who've been shot, taken just after they died on the firing range. How vile can they get! Fortunately, with God's help, Gaston came through the ordeal.

May 19th

My feast day, the day of St Yves, and I have had a great treat. Gaston came in for a long visit. He is still as brave and as full of faith as ever.

Madame Malfuson, the wife of a Bourges barrister who comes to see me when my parents can't, also came. Müller again told me that he was quite sure that Gaston will be reprieved.

Saturday, May 20th

I started up in panic as soon as I heard the commotion down the corridor. The noise seemed to come and go from a cell a few doors down. I sat there in the dark quite paralysed with my eyes wide open. I prayed as I strained to catch the sounds, and hoped against hope.

There was a long silence, and then I heard the tell-tale rattle of chains and the sound of footsteps approaching. Then came Gaston's firm voice saying, "Goodbye," as he passed my door. I had to gather all my strength to answer him. Franz later came in and stood there staring at me for some time, his eyes red and smarting behind his glasses. Then he shifted his weight awkwardly from one foot to the other, shook his keys nervously, and said hoarsely, "I've got a heart too." He turned away quickly and left so that I should not see him cry, and perhaps to avoid seeing my tears too.

Paul told me about it all: "Your friend was quite extraordinary, you know. He held his head high all the while and never stopped smiling. He said goodbye to everyone he saw on the way just as though he was off on holiday. The others followed him, resigned."

Three of them were killed: Gaston, Martinet, and Moreau.

I have just received his last note, written a few hours before he died. Paul gave it to me with trembling hands, without saying a word. I am sure that Gaston did not know he was to die. He was aware of the proximity of the fatal tenth day, of course, but there were no signs of fear. He says he enjoyed seeing me for such a good long while yesterday, thanks to Paul.

"It was marvellous to return to our private world. I felt for a time I was really settled in there again. We must hope that God will see fit to let us continue our friendship. When we are out of here we shall not be separated all the time as we are now." Alas, dear brother Gaston, we shall never meet again in this life. I wonder if Paul knew beforehand. If he did, he gave Gaston his last moments of joy on this earth. As Gaston used to say, Paul is a good sort.

I have re-read the seventeen notes that Gaston wrote me over the last ten days. He sometimes wrote more than once a day and the warders always saw to it that I got everything he wrote.

For me Gaston is not dead. I feel his presence near me, and I shall never get used to the idea of not seeing him again. I am so wretchedly unhappy, so very sad. When I do get to sleep I dream he is still alive, when I wake I am so alone. He was my very dearest friend. I really loved him. I can't help but cry. There is nothing to savour in life any more.

May 22nd

I shall copy out some extracts from Gaston Roy's notes. They are things he wrote between being sentenced and executed and show the loftiness of his sentiments.

This is how he reacted to the news that his betrayer had been shot on May 13th: "He may have caused a lot of innocent people a lot of suffering and sorrow, but I hope he died a decent Christian death and that Heaven will forgive and receive him. I shall pray for him."

On his own fate: "I have been able to accept my fate calmly. I am quite resigned, though I would not have thought this possible a short while ago. I now feel saved."

Then, farther on: "One should never dwell on one's own personal misfortunes. A look around shows people much worse off than oneself."

June 5th

Jacques and Guy Drancourt drove over from their estate at Gien to see me. When Müller was out of the room, because he did "not want to eavesdrop", Jacques turned to me and said, "We're taking you back with us. We drove down on the gas-producer, but I've brought a good supply of petrol."

I managed to convince them that it just could not be done, and that we were all likely to die in the attempt. They were reluctant to leave me and gave me a long, lingering, farewell look, as though for the last time. I probably dissuaded them because I haven't got the guts to escape, because their Viva Grand Sport can easily do a good seventy-five even on the gas-producer. Müller came in looking surprised, "I thought you'd be gone," he said. "We would have covered up for you for a few days."

What an incredible fellow! As a matter of fact, I have met four incredible people while in prison: Schultz and Basedow are incredible for their sadism and cruelty; Alfred and Müller are incredible for their devoted courage and love of their fellow men.

June 6th

Joseph brought me the sweeping brush at seven o'clock and said, "They've landed."

Later he came to tell me more. They landed last night at Cherbourg, Rouen, Le Havre, Dieppe, Dunkirk, Lorient, the Côte d'Azure, Nice, Clermont, Royat, Riom, la Courtine, and God knows where else.

There's no more electricity, no more newspapers.

June 9th

A letter from Marc. They started for home in the afternoon and arrived the following morning. Their journey was "interrupted by constant strafing from dive-bombers. We had to keep leaping into ditches to take cover. We had to walk down the track for miles. In places the rails were blasted off their sleepers and twisted up into the air. Whole parts of trains including entire engines were blown on to rooftops. It was a real nightmare," he writes.

There are no trains running, so Heaven only knows when I shall see Mother and Marc again.

The Gestapo are working round the clock. The whole of Bourges and its surrounding suburbs appear to be passing through the Bordiot. The prison empties and fills up again daily.

I am in good company. I have a major in the gendarmes with me, a deputy mayor, and a police officer.

There are no more civilian trains, but the Gestapo wagons roll on. Their filthy work has priority.

[XII]

In June Yves was allowed no more visits, but we still had news from him, thanks to Müller who got mail through despite the postal chaos.

We were very worried when Bourges was bombed, but messages from Müller again reassured us.

At the end of July 1944, after the Avranches breakthrough when Patton's Army swept through the gap, we lost contact with Bourges. We were scared stiff. Trains stopped running. The railway lines and the roads were under constant fire. The telephone and mail systems were paralysed. Our delight at the Allies' lightning advances was tempered by our anxiety as to the effects it would have on the Wehrmacht, and the Gestapo in particular. We had heard that the Allies' progress had in many cases been disastrous for a lot of Frenchmen.[1] The Gestapo in their panic

---

[1] In August 1944 forty-nine maquis men in Troyes prison were taken from their cells and shot in front of graves dug in the chalk of the Créney firing range.

Then there was the tragedy at the wells of Guerry in 1944. It was one of the most horribly pointless crimes of the War. The FFI was rather too hasty in liberating the town of Saint-Amand-Montrond in the early part of July. The Germans marched back and retook the area, and then decided to punish the inhabitants for their collaboration. They and the militia instigated a large-scale round-up of Alsace-Lorraine Jews, refugees who had been living in Saint-Amand since 1940. The Bourges Gestapo were put in charge of the operation. Hasse was given command and was helped by Basedow, Winterling, Emmerich, and the vile Paoli. Seventy-one Jews —twenty-seven men, thirty-five women, and nine children—were loaded into lorries and piled into the Bordiot on July 28th.

The Gestapo chief at Orleans ordered them to be liquidated, so the men were piled back into the lorries and driven to a quiet corner of the artillery range near Guerry farm. They were unloaded in batches of six. Winterling loaded each one with a bag of solidified cement, and they were placed on the edge of one of the deep wells. The Gestapo men then pushed them in one by one, but before they fell in they were made to drop their bag of cement on top of the previous man wallowing in the waters below. Twenty-eight men met their deaths in this way on July 28th, and eight women

[149]

were goaded into perpetrating even viler deeds, and the Oradour-sur-Glane incident was still fresh in everyone's minds. The silence and loss of contact was a great strain. We could not know what had happened or was happening to Yves. Had he been deported, like the prisoners from Fresnes? Even at Saint-Germain the occupying forces were getting nervous, and I was picked up one evening in a raid for no reason at all and held for an hour at the German HQ. Only my knowledge of German saved me.

When the Allies landed in Provence on August 15th the German occupation began to collapse. Guy, who had been hiding in Paris for weeks, finally came home. The two of us, together with our Resistance friends, started preparing for the liberation. We would meet in the evenings, check our weapons, allot tasks, and make contact with the FFI. We were at last doing what we had longed to do for so many years. They were exciting and rewarding days, but our happiness was clouded by our ignorance of Yves's fate and whereabouts. Mother busied herself sewing FFI armbands for our group and repairing our uniforms.

On August 21st the Germans vanished from Saint-Germain without firing a single shot. An isolated motor-cycle patrol did wend its lonely way through the rue de Pontoise, whereupon we immediately opened fire, to no effect whatever. We occupied all the main vantage points: the barracks, town hall, and the police station where ancient, pot-bellied policemen issued us with half a dozen Lebel rifles (of pre-1914 vintage) and a few antique revolvers.

Several of us were then involved in an incident that might have proved disastrous for us all. On the banks of the Seine, opposite the isle of Andrésy, a handful of our FFI, armed to the teeth with antique weapons, faced a German company entrenched on the far bank of the river, who pounded us roundly with heavy guns. I knew we would be done for if we did not get some help quickly, so I took it upon myself to rush off and ask for help from the Americans, whose advance parties were coming up fast.

were murdered in the same way down another Guerry well on August 8th. Only one, a Jewish tradesman named Charles Kraméïsen, managed to escape and live to tell the tale of this revolting massacre. He was prosecution witness at Paoli's trial.

The American Fifth Armoured Division had knocked the heart out of the XII Panzer Division by the end of July by their pincer movement round Mortain. It was part of General Hodges' First Army, hot on the heels of the fleeing Germans who had escaped the Falaise trap. That warm evening of August 22nd the Fifth Armoured Division had temporarily lost sight of the enemy and were resting up while they waited for fresh petrol supplies. They were between Mantes and Orgeval on the left bank of the Seine. The tank men of the 10th Battalion were lying in the orchards while the gunners were shooting their 105's at random targets to the north of the river for practice.

Captain Mark S. Lillard with his inseparable friend Captain Paul E. Weber decided to take a jeep and reconnoitre the area east of their position, towards Saint-Germain. At a place called "La Maison Blanche", at the crossroads with the road to Villennes, they encountered a cyclist sporting a tricolour arm-band over his not quite military uniform, struggling along on a lady's bicycle with a flat back tyre. I was the first English-speaking FFI they had ever met and they were my first Americans. The captains greeted me in true Yankee style with many a slap on the back, many a Chesterfield cigarette, and more K-rations. They took me to the officer commanding the 10th Tank Battalion, Lieutenant-Colonel Hamberg, a short, stocky man of Dutch descent who shouldered his considerable responsibilities admirably for a man of thirty-two. He listened carefully to what I had to say, and then ordered his practising gunners to switch their fire to the spot where our Germans were entrenched. Under this efficient assault the Germans soon pulled out of Andrésy.

The Lieutenant-Colonel's command post was a half-track vehicle bristling with radio transmitters and receivers all madly buzzing and sizzling and cracking, with "Charlie" answering "Roger" and vice versa, interspersed with many a whistle and whine and the occasional blast of jazz. One really had to be quite some expert to make any sense of that complex cacophony. Lieutenant-Colonel Hamberg came straight to the point: "We need a Frenchman to scout ahead of the division and make contact with the FFI. So how about being liaison officer for my battalion?" I was thrilled. It was like a dream coming true. I had longed for such an opportunity ever since I left cavalry

[151]

school at Saumur, where we were taught the main doctrine of
our arm: "The cavalry scouts, protects, and fights."

I accepted eagerly, whereupon Captain Weber gave me his
own parachute boots, a battledress, helmet, and tommy-gun.
Lieutenant-Colonel Hamberg thought that as I was not in the
regular French Army I would be taking quite a risk, so he
drafted me into the United States Forces and pinned on my
shirt collar the badges of an American second lieutenant!

I spent my first night behind the American lines lying under
a half-track in the dew. The events of the past few months kept
me awake. I kept thinking of Yves. He would have loved to be
with me on the eve of our triumphant entry into Saint-Germain.
My two new friends, Lillard and Weber, were endlessly curious
about France, the Occupation, and my Bourges adventures.
They were nice, straightforward, uncomplicated men, giving
to the war the same zest and vigour they would have given a good
game of basketball. Mark Lillard was twenty-eight but he looked
older. His hair was close cropped and already grey, he wore
rimless glasses, and had a long, intelligent, ascetic face, which
made him look like Pope Pius XII. He was from Jacksonville,
Florida, but worked as an engineer in Detroit. Paul Weber was
his opposite. He was podgy, pink, and fair, but nimble in spite of
his build and very good-natured. He worked in a Connecticut
bank and was the same age as me, twenty-seven.

With these two fellows I lived through a hundred exciting
adventures during the French campaign of September 1944
that took us to the very threshold of Germany. We were covered
in glory when we liberated Saint-Germain. We were treated like
war-lords and heroes. Then there was the gregarious welcome
Paris accorded us as we took part in the victory march. It was like
a large-scale Bastille Day celebration. Clusters of people clung
to our half-tracks, the tanks rumbled past, and the crowd
jumped amid the clouds of petrol exhaust fumes which they had
not smelt for such a long time. It was with Lillard and Weber that
I fought in the forest of Compiègne, where I narrowly escaped
death on two occasions. Every tree concealed a sniper, and the
U.S. Air Force was eventually called in to flatten anything
that moved. In their company I saw the people of the north cry
for joy and the Belgian crowds exult. Together we witnessed

OF BOURGES

what Caesar in 57 B.C. described as the "furious ardour" of the people of Remi whose joy at being liberated was touched with a certain sorrow. We drove through Luxembourg's densely wooded valleys whose thick undergrowth represented a real hazard to our fast tanks. Together we saw Ettelbruck go up in flames and it was our combat team which took Diekirch. I was with them in Diekirch when I captured a booby-trapped Mercedes, and when I had disconnected the wires and made it safe it was promptly presented to me by Colonel Hamberg.

I was also with them when Paul Weber's head was blown off his shoulders by a mortar shell. We were having breakfast near the Siegfried Line. And it was Captain Lillard's manly grief, his lean, wolf's face ravaged by tears, that is the last vivid memory I have of my brief service in the American Army.

When Paul Weber died I went to see Colonel Hamberg and said, "Like all the rest of us, I stayed up all last night thinking of Paul's death. I also had a sort of premonition. I've been thinking about my brother a lot and, as you know, I don't know whether he's alive or in prison or what. But last night I had a feeling that he's on his way home, and I'd like to go back to Saint-Germain and find out if there's any news. I would rather go than remain to wonder and worry about him. The Mercedes you so kindly gave me will get me home. May I have your permission to leave?"

The Colonel consented immediately. He gave me jerrycans of petrol and wrote me a very flattering discharge, and then I went round saying goodbye to everyone, embracing my friend Mark Lillard like a brother.

I made for Paris over the torn-up roads, and the nearer I got to Paris the more convinced I was that Yves would soon be home.

I arrived in Saint-Germain-en-Laye in the evening of September 13th. Guy had joined the Leclerc Division and was on forty-eight-hour leave. My parents were very anxious about Yves as there was no news from Bourges and it had not been mentioned on the wireless. Their pleasure at my return was marred by this constant feeling of apprehension, but I managed to pass on to them some of my own optimism.

"I tell you, he'll soon be home. It won't be long now."

[153]

The next morning at eight o'clock we heard familiar footsteps on the garden path. It was Yves!

"What did I tell you? He's back!"

Mother's incredible joy, Father's enormous relief, everyone's sheer happiness . . . I cannot describe what it was like.

Mother seemed to regain all the weight she had lost since his trial, the colour flooded back into her cheeks, and her gentle blue eyes laughed again and filled with joyful tears.

Yves was very calm and had not changed much, except that he was paler and thinner and had grown a Clark Gable moustache that made him look older. The house was soon flooded by neighbours and friends who had helped and comforted us during the past year: the Allinnes, the Sarrus, the Latours, the Malavallons, the Lamares, the Scheideckers . . .

Yves was showered with questions, but his first need was for something to eat as he had had nothing for two days. The American rations came in handy.

"Well," he said at last, "from the beginning of August everything started happening pretty quickly. The Germans realized the game was up and started scouting about for alibis, just in case the worst came to the worst. They tidied everything up and tried to make us believe we had been well treated—they were desperate to clear themselves of blame. The Gestapo were the first to leave, and until they went I was really scared, but they were gone by August 6th. On August 17th I was called to the visiting room to talk to the colonel in charge of the Bourges sub-area. He was very charming and polite and even offered me a seat. 'Monsieur Tolédano,' he said solemnly, 'it is my pleasure to inform you that in view of your dignified and courageous conduct since you were sentenced to death, I have decided to release you. You have a free pardon. I hope you will appreciate the difference between the German Army and the Gestapo and that you will not forget what I am doing for you. There is, however, one condition: you must be clear of Bourges within six hours. Well, goodbye and good luck.'

"I needed no further encouragement, but grabbed my few belongings, said goodbye to Müller,[1] and shook hands with Paul

---

[1] Müller, that good, understanding, cultivated friend, was killed a few days later for a cause he abominated.

and Frantz. Then I ran to see Maître Malfuson, who gave me an enormous meal. I hid in Bourges for three weeks, sleeping in different places every night, and it was amazing how many people were ready to help. As there were no trains, no mail, no phones, nothing, I couldn't think how to get word to you.

"On September 4th there was a battle at Les Aix d'Aigillon and the FFI rounded up a large group of Germans. On the 6th the FFI, under Colonel Colomb, guided by Georges Ruetsch, liberated Bourges. Oh, Marc, if only you'd been there—it was terrific. I went to a *Te Deum* in the cathedral on the 10th and it was marvellous. Then yesterday I managed to get a lift with a couple of parachutists going to Paris. We drove all through the night and here I am."

Mother hung on his words excitedly and then said simply, "I knew God would not forsake you."

Father turned to her and, paraphrasing Péguy, said proudly, though without boasting, "Here are your sons who have fought so well."

But there was still a cloud on the horizon—Alfred. "Do you know what has happened to him?" asked Mother. "It's such a pity he's not with us today."

"I haven't heard of him since he left the Bordiot four months ago," said Yves.

"He's such a wily old fox though," I said, "and he'll have made so many friends in Dijon, that he's bound to be safe and sound."

On April 4th our Franciscan had said goodbye to the prisoners in the Bordiot and to all his friends in Bourges. He had been promoted to sergeant and sent on to the Dijon prison. At the time, some thought that Alfred had finally become suspect and that his transfer was a disciplinary measure, but this explanation seems unlikely on two counts. Had they really suspected him, punishment would have been harsh. Then his transfer was accompanied by promotion and promotion and rank were held in the greatest esteem by the highly disciplined and disciplinary body that was the German Army. An NCO had very special privileges and a thorough investigation into Alfred's qualifications would have preceded such a promotion. It may be extraordinary but nonetheless it is true that the Franciscan was never suspected by the Gestapo.[1] In fact, the longer Alfred stayed at the Bordiot the greater and stronger became the peculiar "conspiracy of silence" that grew around him. He won over the entire prison guard detachment. They were all behind him. The captain in charge had known of his comings and goings and, if he had not actively encouraged them, at least he turned a blind eye. Kurt Michel, that rather limited Alsatian, was the only rotten apple and he was sent elsewhere.[2] The warders were not all prime examples of human kindness but they were not a bad lot really.

Alfred's supremely gentle and humane nature, and his Christian motives and convictions, affected them all, and when he left his work was carried on by another great-hearted German, the interpreter Müller. Alfred Stanke was a man alone in a hostile environment. He ran the risk of being caught, of slipping up, of being betrayed by jealous colleagues. Had he been discovered he would have been clapped into irons and flung into a Gestapo dungeon: the gallows or the firing squad were always just a slip or two away. And yet he carried on calmly fulfilling his mission for sixteen perilous months. It was during his stay that the Gestapo penetrated the Resistance networks with their double agents and rent them asunder. But they never looked under their own noses.

It must be remembered that Alfred was not a chaplain but a corporal medical orderly who doubled as a warder, and had all the usual duties of a German soldier. An Army chaplain in a prison had specific functions and duties and his work was clear for all to see. Without minimizing in any way the wonderful work done by Father Franz Stock, the German chaplain at Fresnes prison, it is true to say that it cannot be compared with what Alfred accomplished. Such comparisons, however, are odious, for the exercise of charity should not and cannot be evaluated. Stanke's duties were theoretically confined to the dispensing of the occasional aspirin for colds and of syrup of

[1] Proof of this is that Paoli, at his trial, was genuinely astonished to learn of Alfred's work and those present will never forget the look of sheer hatred and cold rage that came into the traitor's eyes at this knowledge.
[2] He was killed on the Russian front.

figs for bowel trouble, and he was strictly forbidden to give succour to the beaten, the tortured, and the dying. And yet he managed to save lives and souls with a little mercurochrome and a vast reserve of love and kindness.

Alfred was forced to do his work in the dark. He had no alternative but to risk his life if he was to give help to the suffering. He succeeded in smoothing away the feeling of collective hatred that existed, while the war was still being waged. That was quite some accomplishment when one considers how much time and energy it has taken us to forgive and forget during peace-time. It is hard now to think oneself back into that atmosphere of loathing and violence that rose out of the horrific crimes committed in the Cher region and elsewhere. That was what Alfred had to contend with and that was what he dissipated in all who came into contact with him. I can safely say that every single person that passed through Bordiot between December 1942 and April 1944—and there must have been at least a thousand for Paoli alone arrested over three hundred in eight months—was helped by Alfred. Many were saved from death and deportation by his efforts. Others were given a new lease on life by his acts of generosity, consideration, and affection. The simple gesture of giving a man an apple during his exercise time, or hiding some piece of personal property to avoid searches and confiscation, can restore prisoners' hopes and spirits. Others were rescued by alibis he furnished, by pre-interrogation advice: "Whatever happens, never admit to anything, always say no . . . you never listened in to the English radio, your friend never confessed to anything of the kind . . . never let the Gestapo intimidate you or get the better of you . . ." Then there were the letters and bits of scribbled paper that Alfred would stuff into his pockets and deliver safely and, thanks to an infallible visual memory, he never once confused the recipients. He took it upon himself to go and warn parents and friends in and around Bourges and Vierzon, and he even went as far afield as Paris and Belfort. He arranged for prisoners to communicate with each other, he bought food and cigarettes with his own money to distribute to prisoners on his rounds. His physical demeanour alone communicated hope and love: his firm warm handshake, the frank honesty of his mischievous eyes, his jolly smile, and the simple, cheering, sincere words of encouragement that came straight from his heart. He had the effect of restoring one's courage and hope and faith.

When Alfred left the Bordiot it was calamity for the Bourges network which he had created with his trustworthy friends—the Farencs, Desgeorges, Abbé Moreux, Ruetsch, Colonel Haegelen, Férandon, d'Ambert, and so many others. When he was gone they had no way of passing mail. Félix Desgeorges tried to revive the network within the prison and failed. Alfred Stanke was irreplaceable. The Desgeorges group were apparently unaware of Müller's rabid anti-Nazism or they would have made good use of it.

The world will never be able to pay sufficient homage to men like Félix Desgeorges and Georges Ruetsch for their devoted Resistance work. There were a lot of people in Bourges who did not know—for obvious reasons—of their secret activities and who labelled them "collaborators" because of their close contact with the Germans. Georges Ruetsch was the interpreter at the local German HQ, while Alfred was a regular guest of the Desgeorges household. Georges Ruetsch's very work made him the vital link in the group because he had ready access to information and could thus keep Alfred and the Resistance informed as to the Germans' plans. The loyal Desgeorges had been arrested at the beginning of the Occupation, but he had managed to win the confidence of his earlier captors by supplying them with drink. The hustle and bustle of Germans about his wine shop in the rue Jean-Baffier enabled Alfred to come and go and do his business without ever incurring the slightest suspicion from his superiors.

Alfred started all over again at Dijon. The Dijon Gestapo was large and very strong because of the strength and number of the local maquis groups. Resistance men were rounded up in great droves and ran the usual gauntlet of torture and suffering. The prison in the rue d'Auxonne acquired more and more prisoners daily. After the Normandy landing the firing squads were on duty round the clock and packed trains carted endless loads of deportees off to Germany. Alfred gave himself to these poor devils in the same way as he had at Bourges. When General Tarnier was secretly put in the condemned cell it was Alfred who saved him from execution. Hundreds of others benefited from his unflagging help, like Abbé Court who ran the local youth club in the rue de Mulhouse, Police Inspector Jeoffroy, and Resistance men such as Iermann and Troncin. It was with Troncin that Alfred set up his Dijon mail system.

He continued to place himself at risk and court death—in fact, his daring seemed to know no bounds. He would filch incriminating papers, hide prisoners in the sick bay to save them being deported, warn Charles Troncin that on a certain day seven men were going to be shot and that he should mount a rescue operation, and so on. He even demanded that a French interpreter be punished because his excessive zeal had been making life more difficult for the prisoners.

It was through this interpreter that Alfred was very nearly, caught, the narrowest escape of his life. One day a young woman gave the interpreter a letter for her husband in prison. The interpreter asked Alfred to pass it on to the husband, but the wary Franciscan was always on his guard. "Do your own errands," he said. Alfred insisted, however, that the letter should not remain in the man's cell and that he should give it up to the interpreter when he had finished reading it. But the interpreter did not ask for the letter back and the inevitable happened. The Gestapo was alerted and they searched the husband's cell, found the letter, and arrested the woman. Alfred was implicated, quite probably by the interpreter. The husband was tortured but refused to accuse Alfred, insisting that he had not received the letter from a German. The Gestapo then beat up the woman and made her file past a parade of soldiers and identify the culprit. She lingered before Alfred for what seemed like an age, during which time Alfred experienced something like a homicidal urge. But the girl shook her head and passed on. Alfred was saved, but suspect, and from then on he was closely watched. He became more circumspect. When it was clear by mid-August that Germany was collapsing the officer in charge of the prison called Alfred and advised him to throw away his uniform and make his getaway. Alfred refused, though he could easily have taken refuge perfectly safely, for his many friends among the priests in Dijon and Bourges would have protected and sheltered him. Many a Resistance man on the Côte d'Or or in

[159]

the Cher district would have considered it both an honour and a duty to harbour Brother Alfred. But he refused. He would not abandon his fellow German soldiers in their hour of need. He wanted to share their fate now that the tables had turned, for they might benefit from his help.

The FFI who captured him on September 15th, 1944, near Vesoul never learnt about his invaluable services to captured Frenchmen, nor did Alfred choose to enlighten them. Just before he was taken prisoner Alfred heard from a fleeing Bourges warder that Yves had been set free. Alfred was really thrilled when he heard that the condemned man of whom he had grown so fond was now safe and sound.

He was handed over to the Americans and after a stint at Saint-Raphaël and a long transit journey across North Africa, he was sent as a prisoner of war to the United States.

He lived the humdrum life of the prison camps in Idaho and Arizona, and devoted all the energy and affection he had once given patriotic Frenchmen to his fellow German prisoners.

He did not, however, forget all his French friends and often wondered what had become of all the men he had known who had been deported to Germany. He, like everyone in the United States, got to know of the hideous crimes committed at Dachau, Auschwitz, Mathausen, Dora, Oranienburg, Treblinka, Bergen-Belsen, Buchenwald, Struthof, and other such revolting places, and it broke his heart.

Epilogue

The people of Bourges did not forget their Franciscan and they immediately started to trace him. Former inmates of the Bordiot who loved Alfred and were concerned about his welfare brought his case before the Berry Remembrance Committee. The Committee initiated proceedings to obtain his release and bear public witness to the vast debt so many men owed him.

In 1945 the Cher Liberation Committee sent the following petition to the American authorities signed by a Communist Member of Parliament:

> The Cher liberation Committee has investigated the case of Aloïse Stanke, known as "Alfred", a warder and medical orderly working in Bourges prison during the Occupation, and has collected and examined evidence brought forward by former prisoners.
>
> It has been proved that this warder's conduct towards prisoners was exemplary. We have proof that he enabled political detainees to communicate within the prison and without. We have proof that it was through his personal intervention that many prisoners were able to prepare an effective defence before their trial by either the Gestapo or a German military court and were thus spared the death sentence.
>
> The Committee wishes to associate itself with the wishes and desires expressed by these numerous witnesses that have come forward in requesting the immediate release of Aloïs Stanke, at present held prisoner in New York (Prisoner of War Camp Fearragut, Box 20, personal number 9. WG. 8094).
>
> Certified a true copy.
>
> MARCEL CHERRIER
Vice-President

On June 18th, 1946, Alfred was finally released and Bourges started preparing a royal reception for him.

On June 6th, 1947, Georges Ruetsch, who was then serving as a lieutenant in the French Army of Occupation at Baden-Baden, led an official delegation to seek out Alfred in his Heidelberg monastery and take him to Bourges, where he arrived on June 11th and was received by two hundred former prisoners and their families.

He looked much better in his dignified rough brown habit than he had in that hideously tight German army uniform. He was very deeply moved by the unexpected pleasure of seeing so many old friends and shook hands with and embraced everyone. Many were absent because they had left their bones in Germany or had died on the firing range during the final Gestapo panic.

Alfred wept quite openly. He was such a modest and humble soul that he could not quite understand that all the fuss and ceremony was for him and in his honour.

"It's all too much, far too much for a simple Franciscan like me. I only did my duty and acted in the spirit of the habit I wear."

There was a formal reception at the Town Hall where Alfred was presented to the Deputy of the district, the Prefect, and the Mayor, and he had an audience with the Archbishop. He had to sit through several speeches that paid homage to his kindness, generosity, and self-sacrifice.

Then at the end of two days of continual homage and thanks the humble monk returned to his monastery infirmary. He had been moved, touched, and pleased by all the excitement, which had worn him out more than his thirteen months at the Bordiot, and he went back to Germany a happy, proud man. His work and the thanks that had been paid him paved the way for future gestures and efforts of reconciliation. Here was one man whose active existence could eradicate the horrors committed by Himmler's henchmen, by all the Hasses, the Basedows,[1] the Schultzes, the Yeskes, and the Annie Fuhrmanns. He wiped the slate clean.

---

[1] Ernst Basedow, Bourges torturer, was tried by the military court at Lyons in 1950 and was sentenced to ten years' solitary confinement with hard labour. The State Commissioner appealed against the sentence as being unduly lenient.

Alfred's work and brotherly love had not been in vain. What
Christ said in the Gospel Parable of the Talents could equally
apply to Alfred: "Well done, thou good and faithful servant;
thou hast been faithful over a little, but I will set thee over
much. Enter thou into the joy of thy lord."

Postscript

A letter from Monsieur Arnaud de Vogüé[1]

April 20th, 1965

MY DEAR TOLÉDANO,

Thank you kindly for sending me a part of the manuscript of
your memoirs describing the critical point in your life when
you were arrested by the Bourges Gestapo, tortured, and held
for months in the Bordiot prison with your younger brother
Yves.

I have just finished reading it at one sitting, and as I turned
the pages I came across many familiar names which revived
memories of Bourges in the Occupation.

To begin with, there is the picture of that sinister building, the
lair of the Berry Gestapo in the rue Michel-de-Bourges. We
found the place in an incredible state when we entered it on
Liberation Day, after the Gestapo had abandoned it at the end
of August 1944, still bearing traces of the ghastly scenes it had
witnessed for four years.

Then you describe your stay in the Bordiot after undergoing
the most vile tortures. So many of our men suffered in the
Bordiot between 1940 and 1944, and it acquired such a dreadful reputation and was associated with so many horrible memories, that we all hoped the ugly monster would be torn down,
never to admit another Frenchman again after the Germans
left.

Many of your fellow detainees were important Resistance
workers, while many were obscure, unknown sufferers, but your
memoirs rightly deal with them all equally. They were all
patriots joined in the common bond of love for their country, a
sentiment which sustained them in their darkest hours and even
gave them the strength to face the firing squads.

---

[1] Monsieur Arnaud de Vogüé, under the name of Colonel Colomb, commanded the French Forces of the Interior in the northern zone of the Cher
département from February 1944 onwards.

Your memoirs also bring out the strong comradeship which the prisoners in the Bordiot shared with each other. That, and the Christian charity embodied in the humble person of the Franciscan Brother Alfred, the German Army medical orderly, were unique feelings in those violent days.

Brother Alfred is an example to all men. For two years he tended and relieved people's physical and spiritual sufferings. His life and conduct are a fine illustration of Saint Paul's words to Corinthians, "Charity is patient, is kind, charity . . . beareth all things, believeth all things, hopeth all things, endureth all things, Charity never falleth away . . ."

Your testimony, my dear Tolédano, is worthy of a man who has the right to describe what he has undergone and seen.

The readers of your memoirs will never be able to forget the picture you have recreated of the Franciscan of Bourges, of that gentle, godly man who radiated such goodness among the dreadful scenes of horror that took place in Berry during the Occupation.

ARNAUD DE VOGÜÉ

Appendices

Abbé Barut

Abbé Barut's story is worth recounting. In November 1942 Abbé Jean Barut, a Swiss national, decided to visit his mother in Geneva. He was thirty at the time, a healthy, energetic man and a dynamic, vigorous clergyman. He smuggled himself across the Occupied Zone frontier and equally illegally across the border into Switzerland. On December 6th he decided it was time to return to his parish. The easiest way back seemed to be by swimming across the Cher but when he reached the river it was in flood and overflowing its banks. Undeterred, he took off his clothes, rolled them into a bundle, strapped them to his head, and swam over to the opposite bank, which was occupied territory. The water was ice-cold and, having no towel, he rubbed himself down with his shirt, which he then stuffed into his pocket (he was wearing civilian clothes). Then he ran into a German patrol, who would have let him pass on had they not noticed that his chest was not only bare but wet, which they naturally thought unusual for mid-December. They searched him and found his wet shirt, so he was handed over to the Bourges Gestapo and instantly accused of participation in the Resistance. Schultz and his cronies set to work on him to make him "confess" and though he stood his ground firmly, so did the Gestapo.

Meanwhile, Alfred had returned from leave. "In Cell 72 is a terrorist priest," said his superior. "Get him to wash and shave off his beard, but that's all. You are forbidden to have anything else to do with him, you hear?"

Their first meeting did not go well. Alfred walked into his cell and cheerfully told him in French, "Hey, Billy-Goat Pastor, you shave off beard."

"Get the bloody hell out of here, you lousy Boche," shouted the angry Abbé in German, and pushed Alfred out.

The second meeting was more successful. Alfred returned a little later, reluctant to admit defeat. "Pastor, write letter, here are stamps and paper," he said.

[167]

"I told you to get out. As for your stamps, stuff them—"

"Please, not be angry. I too am a Pastor."

"You, a priest! Don't make me laugh!"

"Yes, yes, I am. I am even a Franciscan."

"All right, recite the *Confiteor*, all of it. We'll soon see if you're a Franciscan."

To the Abbé's great astonishment Alfred said the *Confiteor* off pat and included the vital "Sancto Francesco", which proved to the Abbé that he was genuine.

From that moment on they became close friends. Alfred, who had probably been tipped off by Ruetsch about the charges that were going to be brought against the Abbé, advised the priest to write to the Swiss ambassador and told him what to say next time he was interrogated. He also arranged for the Abbé's companion to be a Polish priest, so that the two could hear each other's confessions.

One day a group of Jews arrived in the Bordiot. Everything had been taken away from them and they had been beaten up and their teeth broken by Hasse and his henchmen. Alfred appealed to all the prisoners for help, and Abbé Barut was the first to give up his bread ration to help these poor people. Alfred personally took the Abbé's letter to the Swiss Embassy in Paris. This letter resulted in Barut's eventual release, after a threatening injunction by the Swiss Diplomatic Service. The Gestapo were wild with rage and held a thorough inquiry to try to uncover the Abbé's "accomplice". They were convinced that their captive was a vital link in the Resistance network, and they only yielded him up upon special orders from their superiors at the main Gestapo HQ in the rue des Saussaies.

The Abbé's first-hand experience of German brutality and all he witnessed being done to others had an unexpected result. Until he was arrested he was simply a Swiss subject devoted to his ministerial responsibilities; he had avoided any involvement in the Resistance. When he left the Bordiot, however, he became a fierce opponent of the Germans and an enthusiastic Resistance worker.

Abbé Barut is now the parish priest at Eaubonne (Seine-et-Oise).

Monsieur Bicyclette

This was Alfred's nickname for Monsieur Lerale, a bicycle dealer in Bourges, whose name Alfred found hard to pronounce. He was an active member of the "Vengeance" Group and was arrested in March 1944 with several other members: André Berniot, Serge Noizat, Delias, Guérineau, Roger Péras. Monsieur Lerale was tossed into his cell like a bundle of dirty laundry, dying from a crushed kidney. Alfred took such good care of him that he literally brought him back to life. Through Georges Ruetsch he warned Lerale's wife to destroy all incriminating papers, and then, throwing caution to the winds, actually went to see her in their shop and told her what to say to the Gestapo. The poor woman was arrested by Paoli, but Alfred's warnings and advice saw her through the interrogation. Madame Lerale shared Cell 22 with Madame Fourré and Madame Chauve, the latter having been arrested as a hostage for her son. Alfred took all sorts of trouble and risks to make imprisonment more bearable for these three women, helping them make contact with their husbands and bringing them parcels. If they did not give up in despair it was because of his constant attention.

Edmé Boiché

Edmé Boiché, a Berry man of twenty-two, was a defaulter from the STO (conscripted labour for Germany organized by the Vichy Government). He had obtained two identity cards, a German one to show the Vichy police and a French one to show the Germans. On September 9th he was caught in a German round-up but showed them the German card by mistake. The game was up and he was put into Bordiot, where he shared a cell with five French gendarmes who had been sentenced to death for letting a lorry carrying munitions to the maquis past a roadblock. At his first interrogation Boiché was so enraged that he put a judo lock on his torturer and threw him across the room. This piece of self-defence did not commend him to Fritz Schultz, who set four beefy SS men on him to overpower him and thrash the life out of him. He was left on the floor a broken man. They repeated this operation every day for several days. Finally, like everyone else in the Bordiot, Boiché met Alfred.

"You, Monsieur, you Catholic?"

"No. Go to hell," answered Boiché.

Alfred was inured to such rebuffs. He emptied his packet of Gauloises on Boiché's pallet and said, "There. Write a message inside the packet." Edmé Boiché was finally persuaded of Alfred's sincerity and wrote down his fiancée's name and the message, "Send me a shirt and some food."

The following day Alfred returned with a roast leg of veal, some eggs, and a clean shirt to replace the one the Gestapo had ripped to shreds.

Alfred tended his injuries and served as the devoted intermediary between Boiché and his future in-laws, who promptly became Alfred's friends.

Boiché spent thirteen days in the Bordiot, and then was transferred to Paris and imprisoned in the Pépinière barracks, the assembly centre for STO defaulters before they were deported to Germany. When he was taken and locked into a train at the Gare de l'Est due to leave for Germany, he managed to leap free in the commotion of the train's departure. He hid in Paris and then made it back to the Cher area, where he joined the local FFI under the command of Colonel Colomb, with whom he fought for the rest of the War. He took part in the liberation of Bourges in September 1944.

Challes

From May 1943 onwards General Challes was a member of the "Liberation" Resistance Group and commanded the Orléans district. He was betrayed by a Gestapo double-agent who had joined his group. He and his two sons were arrested in September 1943. On October 8th the other heads of the "Liberation" Group for Bourges were duly picked up: Sadrin, a civil engineer, Bourliaud, a tradesman, and André Pontoizeau, a primary-school inspector and the group's military organizer. These three men were dreadfully tortured by the Gestapo, Pontoizeau being treated to the Berlin top and the leaded pipe, as I was. The group ended up in the Bordiot where they came under Alfred's care and attention. He did all he could to relieve their pain and restore their morale. On October 17th they were transferred to Orléans and from there to Germany, first to

Buchenwald and then to Dora. André Pontoizeau, who managed by some miracle to survive Dora, wrote a book on the camp called *Dora-la-Mort*, in which he describes the appalling hell on earth the inmates were made to endure. My very dear friend Lieutenant Hubert Challes lived just long enough to be freed. He died of exhaustion in May 1945 in the very aeroplane that was bringing him home to Orly.

Pierre-Marie Paoli

The traitor Pierre-Marie Paoli, one of the most cruel and sadistic of all the torturers at Bourges, was born at Aubigny-sur-Nère in the department of Cher on December 31st, 1921. His father, who was of Corsican descent, was a herbalist, while his mother was a milliner. In 1938 he was a temporary clerk in the taxation offices at Mehun-sur-Yèvre. When the Germans occupied France, he decided that his future lay in their camp, and on March 31st, 1943, he got himself a job as an interpreter with Bourges Gestapo. His enthusiasm did not pass unnoticed and he was promoted rapidly, but he soon realized where his true talents lay and became one of their principal murderer-torturers. He had a twisted mind that conceived of the most excrutiating and repulsive methods of torture: ripping off fingernails, peeling off skin in strips, burning the extremities, hanging victims up by their feet, gradual electrocution, bathtub immersions, and so on. These acts of devotion to the Nazi cause were intended to, and did, ingratiate him with the Gestapo. In a single year well over three hundred people were arrested by Paoli. Most of them were tortured by him, and he killed some with his own two hands. Only a few straggled back from the death camps to which he had sent them. In his home town of Aubigny he arrested twenty-three people, most of whom he had known all his life. Only four of them survived deportation.

The twenty-two-year-old dandy's name was a byword for horror round Bourges. Everyone dreaded crossing his path. An attempt was made on his life in Aubigny itself; he was wounded and was laid up in hospital at Orléans for several months, but when he returned he was ten times viler and more savage than before. Some of his best-known accomplishments were the rounding up of the "Vengeance" Group leaders, the mass arrests at

Baffes where sixty people were horribly treated and deported to Germany, the shooting of several innocent passengers, apparently for the fun of it, in a train which he had stopped at Veaugues in May 1944, and the appalling Guerry wells massacre. The first six months of 1944 were crammed with a horrifying list of crimes, robberies, tortures, sufferings, and tears resulting from his bestiality. He fled to Germany on August 6th, 1944. On his way he kept in practice by stopping in the Ardennes with a bunch of French-speaking false maquis men and some Germans to round up, quite at random, about twenty people. They tortured them horribly and then proceeded to put a gun to their temples and shoot each dead in turn.

On May 16th, 1945, Paoli was arrested by the British military police in Flensburg, near the Danish border, and was handed over to the French police in January 1946. He was condemned to death by the military court at Bourges on May 3rd, 1946, and the sentence was confirmed at a second trial at Nancy a few days later. He was executed on June 15th, 1946, at the Bourges artillery range.

A very unbiased and objective book, *L'Affaire Paoli*, by Jean Lyonnet, a former examining magistrate Departmental Court of the Cher and president of the bench of Auxerre, was published in 1965. It describes the short and bloody career of this killer and gives all the evidence that was brought forward at the trials.

Translators' Notes

Maquis

This was the general name for the French effort to resist the German Occupation from 1940 onwards. Originally it meant the dense oak and chestnut woods with thick, matted undergrowth of heather, arbutus, and wild laurel common in the hilly areas of the Mediterranean. In the late nineteenth and early twentieth centuries, these woods sheltered Corsican bandits and those involved in vendettas, so that "to take to the maquis" eventually came to mean "to take refuge from and oppose established authority". Thus, during the German occupation of France, Frenchmen who dodged labour conscription and men who worked for the eventual overthrow of the Nazis "took to the maquis", where groups would make contact with the Allies and work with them. Two of the main maquis organizations were:

The FTP, Franc-Tireurs et Partisans, mainly a left-wing and Communist organization;

The FFI, Forces Françaises de l'Intérieur, a larger and more broadly-based, less politically orientated organization than the FTP.

Jean Moulin (1899–1943)

He became the Prefect of the Eure-et-Loire Department, and in 1940 he founded the General Council of the Resistance, a centre for co-ordinating the Resistance movements against the Germans. He was arrested by the Gestapo and died in a concentration camp. His remains were recently given a national funeral and then laid to rest in the Panthéon.

Pierre Brossolette (1903–44)

He was a schoolmaster and a historian who then became a journalist and a socialist politician. He was a prime mover in the Resistance. When the Gestapo arrested him he knew so much of such vital importance and was so afraid that he might break under torture that he committed suicide by hurling himself down a stairwell.

Honoré d'Estienne d'Orves (1901–41)

This naval officer was one of the pioneers of the French Resistance. He was shot by the Germans on the infamous Mont Valérien firing range in Paris.